SERMONS AND PRAYERS

SERMONS AND PRAYERS

By

WILLIAM DYGNUM MOSS

*Pastor of the
Presbyterian Church, Chapel Hill
1904-1906, 1912-1932*

A MEMORIAL VOLUME

CHAPEL HILL
THE UNIVERSITY OF NORTH CAROLINA PRESS
1940

COPYRIGHT, 1940, BY
THE UNIVERSITY OF NORTH CAROLINA PRESS

PREFACE

THE PRESENT selection of sermons and prayers was made from a very large number which were typed from manuscript by Miss Mary Broome. To her the Editorial Committee is greatly indebted, and to many friends of Dr. Moss thanks are due for financial support of the publication. It is hoped that the choices made will find favor as representing and reproducing, as far as the printed page can, the Parson's religious philosophy. There is no topical order of presentation; but the calendar of a college year is partially followed.

          F. F. BRADSHAW,
          R. B. HOUSE,
          GEORGE McF. McKIE,
          G. A. HARRER, *Chairman.*

PARSON MOSS

THE MAN AND HIS MINISTRY

By *Francis F. Bradshaw*

WILLIAM DYGNUM MOSS, a native of Canada and an alumnus of McGill University, came to Chapel Hill in 1904 from a pastorate in Nova Scotia. He was turning southward for reasons of health. In 1906 he went to a charge in Washington, D. C. In 1912 he returned to Chapel Hill to a congregation which had refused to be satisfied with any substitute for "the Parson," and here he remained until his death on October 6, 1932.

An alumnus related recently how he, a rebellious youth, had promised himself upon entering the University that he would not attend church a single time while away from home and enjoying the freedom of the collegian. At the opening exercises of the University the Reverend Mr. Moss was asked to pray. An initial sentence was so little like the perfunctory and unthought petitions of custom that the lad felt actually startled—he said, almost as if by a dash of water in the face. He decided to hear the minister the next Sunday, and, although not a Presbyterian, he heard the Parson regularly for four years.

Such was the charm of the minister for hundreds of all denominations that his church was at times almost the University church. The appended extracts from the diary of one of his non-Presbyterian parishioners will serve to illustrate the method and appeal of his campus-wide pastorate. His parishioners were frequently, in good-natured raillery, called the "Mossites." He was the minister most frequently invited to student gatherings, Y. M. C. A. installations, and fraternity house discussion groups; and his Vesper Sermon was made an annual commencement feature for parents and seniors. There was deep significance and feeling in that commencement ceremony when the University designated him her Doctor of Divinity.

To tramp the woods' paths with the Parson, to golf with him, to share a problem with him, to have him meet the best girl and later perform the marriage rites at Piney Prospect or in some distant home town, to keep late vigil with him amid perplexities or pains, such sweet comradeship became a part of the liberal and liberating arts in Chapel Hill.

There was some uniqueness about the man as well as profoundness in the preacher. In the structure of his growth there were many unusual and varied elements. There was a boyhood on the prairies of Manitoba—he was one of a large family on a ranch which included a school, church, trading post, and distillery, in Scottish juxtaposition. The farmer father, who had built this community, added to other roles that of big-game hunter in the Rockies every year. The Parson's stories revealed also the Indian and Chinese characters of this prairie. Then, at the age of fourteen, there was the adventure of a transcontinental trip from home via Chicago to Montreal. Then came the pranks and other forms of humor in the college and the seminary in Montreal.

At his second charge, St. Andrew's in Nova Scotia, he and his session went on fishing trips in the Canadian woods every spring. During the first of the Chapel Hill pastorates he shared the rollicking talk-fests and deep fellowships of the students. His stories of his Washington pastorate included a share in the adventures of the head of the Federal Secret Service, efforts to temper the winds of civil service to the underpaid and overworked, domestic incidents in a fine Italian fruit-store family, and association with the personages and powers of a growing American capital.

Then came tours of the Old World and deep moments with Wordsworth, Keats, and Rossetti. A continuous interest in poetry and philosophy gradually enriched a fine mind. Time brought enough personal suffering to maintain ready sympathy and enough mature perspective to sharpen a quick, though affectionate, eye for the comic.

All these and many more were the threads of experience which made the Parson the kind of person he was. In retrospect one wonders how there could have been developed a better minister to college youth and college community. His Kant and Hegel were as abundantly bethumbed and annotated as his Keats and Rossetti, but only the poetry appeared verbatim in the sermons. His Children's Day sermons, like his personal companionships, were simultaneously adequate to adult, adolescent, and child.

To many a perplexed student mind he made religion and intelligence appear reciprocally necessary. For several campus generations the Parson, Horace Williams, and Ed Graham, as they worked together and quoted each other in chapel, pulpit, and classroom, seemed apostles of some richer synthesis, the emerging basis of a new and native cultural renaissance. In this group, on the horizon of student worship, the Parson was as though "the Word was made flesh and dwelt among us, full of grace and truth."

PARSON MOSS

EXTRACTS FROM THE DIARY OF R. B. HOUSE

VERY EARLY in my sophomore year I dropped into the Presbyterian Church one Sunday evening, not so much to hear the Parson as to vary my program of church-going.

The Parson preached, as nearly as I can remember, on the Principles to Guide One in Reading the Bible. I was entranced by his thought, and light broke over me and in me. The mind of the Parson had me from that time on. I remained till the congregation had gone and got him to give me an analysis of his sermon, which I wrote in the first volume of my diary. His eager readiness to stay with me and make all clear had me from a new angle—that of the artist in personal relations.

I began to soak up all of Parson's preaching I could get. I began to visit him. I was all seriousness and ready to settle all problems. There I came to see another facet of the Parson. He sensed that I was all too serious. He began to talk about fun, humour, salty, witty wisdom. The talk swung around to O. Henry, and he read aloud "The Handbook of Hymen." Thus he knew how to balance me up in my moods.

Seeing my amateur interest in Philosophy, the Parson introduced me to Professor Williams. Rightly sensing that my chief philosophical interest was ethical, he got me to visit with him Mr. Willams's course in Ethics. Here I got much joy out of the discussions, out of watching the Parson make voluminous notes, and out of his interpretative comments, as on one occasion he whispered to me that the secret of the whole thing was unity.

The Parson showed me how to enjoy literature for what it was worth and not confuse it with logic. He was a Rossetti lover and a Wordsworthian. "The Blessed Damozel" moved him so deeply that he could not read it aloud or talk about it very much. But such things of Wordsworth's as "Tintern Abbey," "Intimations of Immortality," and the ode "Composed upon an Evening of Extraordinary Splendour and Beauty" he had absorbed and made a part of his spirit.

His sensing the characteristic of a man, that obstetric hand of his in coaxing such a characteristic to birth and to growth, was Parson, the teacher. The man was an artist in this—the greatest I have seen.

He was an artist in paying attention to the very person he happened to be talking to on the very thing they happened to be talking about. There was in him none of the transition attitude. He never seemed to be wanting to have done with a person, a time, or a thing, as though to get on to something more important. To sense each thing as fine in itself, to sense the inner characteristic of this thing, to give it background, margin, and full swing in its development was part of his artistry in living. He was truly like Christ at the well.

"Don't press," was his motto in golf. "Each moment has all the quality of eternity," seemed to be his philosophy. "Everybody is in a hurry except God," was his comment on reformers and fanatics.

I have met so many people, each one good enough, but nevertheless each one something of an interruption. I wanted him to go so that I could get back to some greater thing with which I was at the time preoccupied. Parson Moss was the great thing in himself, because he dissolved one's own preoccupations, because he had absorbed his own. Life in flower at the moment was the sacrament he brought.

SERMONS

*Wherewithal shall a young man cleanse his way?
By taking heed thereto according to thy word.*
—Psalm 119:9.

THEY WERE puzzled in those days over the problem of living. It is the only problem. All problems center in the problem of living. You start out to run an automobile. It is a problem in living. There is a right way and a wrong way to go about it. If you go the right way about it, you have lived. If you go the wrong way about it, you have not lived in the running of that machine. That is all there is to it.

From day to day there is one task, therefore—to live. Do you realize, you young people, that that is your task?

> " 'Tis life, whereof our nerves are scant . . .
> More life, and fuller, that we want."

This writer is addressing himself to young men. Today, if he were here, he would address himself to young women, too. In those days young women—

and for that matter older women—did not count. Only the man counted then. I often wonder what those men would think if they lived today and saw how important the woman was, especially the young woman.

How are young people to choose their way? How are they to make of life all that it is intended they should? That is the question involved in this writer's question.

Human beings are wonderful. We do not need any other test of their wonderfulness than this: the way so many of them manage to get along and live, when we reflect on how they do not bother their heads about the problem.

A lot of them do not live. They just exist. And the reason of it is that they do not look ahead. They live emotionally. They do not plan. They do not seek out the purpose of their life. They just come here and go along from day to day as though their life were a purposeless thing.

England, today, has a million people who are out of work and are tramping the streets and lying out in the parks. Of course, like all civilizations, there is something the matter with the way the civilization is run. But I am certain there is something the matter with the individuals themselves. They did not get started right. Allowing for environment and heredity all we should, that baby, now a man lying out in the park or tramping the street, made a wrong move one day when he could have made a right move. So he is where he is and how he is. Some cannot help their sorry condition. Circumstances and heredity were too much for them. But so many could have headed off their present state of things.

The Bible is full of the story. In fact, that is the whole story of the Bible—how one human being makes the most of life, and the other makes the worst of it. The very first story in the Bible presents us with the situation. Our first parents failed. They ought to have succeeded, but they did not. Cain and Abel started out. Cain went down in the struggle; and all the way along, the drama is being enacted, until we come to the New Testament. There we have the story of a man who lived, and we go back to him daily for support in this difficult business of living.

How are we to work it out? It will help us to answer this by first asking why it is that we fail? Why does a normal life fail? We will leave out the abnormal—we are all normal here.

Why does a normal life fail? Why will you fail, if you fail? I hope you will not. It is a lack of judgment. It is a failure to think it out and get at the right thing to be done. And so the way to work it out is to think and come to a correct judgment. That is what the Psalmist means when he answers his own question: "Wherewithal shall a young man cleanse his way? By taking heed thereto according to thy word." God's good word awaits us. God is speaking to us, and in order to find out what God has to say to us, we have to listen to him and weigh his words. That is, we have to think it out.

The Catholic does not put it that way. God's word, he says, is committed to the priest and all we have to do is to do what the priest tells us. It is simple obedience to what the priest says. But even then one has to do a little bit of thinking. He has to think as far as the priest thinks in order to get at what the priest tells him.

The Protestant puts it differently. He says God's word is in the Bible and we must do what the Bible says in order to work it out. But a man has to think out what the Bible says. He has to make it his own.

The Psalmist was like Jesus: "Thy word," he says in another place, "have I hid in mine heart, that I might not sin against thee." A word is a thought, a feeling. God's word is God's thought; it is the divine feeling surging within us. "I will meditate in thy precepts," he says in the same Psalm.

That is it. The Kingdom of God is within us. That is the Jesus way of expressing it. There is a divine stirring within us. From the time we get up in the morning until we go to sleep at night, that divine thought, that divine stirring, is within us.

And how shall we cleanse our way of life? By thinking it out. By taking note of this divine stirring within us and finding out the direction it leads. That calls for thinking and the forming of correct judgments on life. It calls for the thinking of God's thoughts after him.

Sometimes we will fail. Sometimes we will interpret the divine message wrong. But most of the time, if we give ourselves a chance, we will find out what God wants of us. We will form correct judgments. "The Spirit beareth witness with our spirit." "The Spirit searcheth all things, yea, the deep things of God." It is the Spirit of truth; and when we are in this royal habitation of this Spirit of truth within us, we cannot help coming to right conclusions on life and right courses of action.

The priest can help us. But he can help us only to think and form conclusions for ourselves. We can decide to let him do our thinking for us, and in that case we will simply fall back on obedience. There will not be anything of our own in the transaction. I am not criticizing this method of living. I am only presenting it to you. If you want to stop at that stage of living—the stage of obedience—well and good. But it is not the final, full stage of living. It is only obedience to a standard of living set up for us by another man.

The Bible will help us, but we have to interpret the Bible. We have to see how it applies in our case. We have to let it shed light on our problem. That means that we have to think it out for ourselves. The word or the thought of God that came to Isaiah or St. John or Jesus comes to you—the same word of God. It helps us to see how Isaiah or St. John or Jesus thought it out. But we must think it out for ourselves.

It is like a man going on a class. The teacher there, of mathematics, makes his statement, but the student does not get far if he only accepts the statement without thinking it through for himself and making the statement his own. The real mathematician is the man who sees his own way through mathematics, taking all the help from the teacher and the textbook he can get. The really successful man at living is the man who tackles his life problems for himself, taking all the help from the Bible, from Isaiah or Jeremiah or St. Luke or Jesus, he can get.

That is the way I see it. It is the way this Psalmist saw it. I feel it is the way Jesus saw it. And starting out from that basis, we should get along gloriously. It is a case of taking heed thereto according to God's thought, God's word.

Do you realize, you young people, that God is speaking to you? Do you realize that he is speaking to you in a very real, vital, practical sense? There is not anything impractical, evanescent, intangible in it. The simplest story of your life is this God story, this story of thinking, this story of truth.

Here is our trouble. Along with God's voice uttering itself within us is another voice. It is the voice of our emotions. So there is our conflict. Our emotions are urging us one way, and our inner, deeper, divine life is urging us the other way.

Then, because it is the easier thing to do, we go with our emotions and let the higher, the divine urge, that divine thought within us, take care of itself. There we are in trouble. Our way which should be cleansed and clear as the noonday sun is disturbed with a lot of things done that should not have been done, and a lot left undone that should have been done.

You have an emotion. Let us say it is a desire to let the lesson you should study wait while you go out for enjoyment. But God is in that transaction. Watch yourself next time you have a disposition to dodge study. You will find that you do not feel right about it. What is that? It is the great, divine voice speaking to you. Now if you listen to that voice, if you think a very little bit, you will sit down and study and keep the desire to loaf in its place. There is a time to loaf, but it is not when God calls you to study. God is very much in that transaction.

This summer a man got into a first-class coach in England with a third-class ticket. It is curious how people want to dodge the censorship when they are traveling and make themselves feel it is all right if they can get away with it. This man got into the first-class coach with a third-class ticket. Nobody came in to ask him about it. All he had to do was to get off at his destination and hand his ticket to the gate keeper and pass along the highway of life and forget.

He did not do it, for he had a little talk with God on his way. In other words, he did some thinking. When you think, you get at the right in your situation. That is God. He thought, and saw the right thing to be done and did it. He told the gate keeper and paid the extra fare and saved his self-respect, kept on good terms with himself.

I heard of a man the other day who did a little real estate business according to the Psalmist's method. A neighbor who was hard up offered him a piece of land for four hundred dollars that was worth a good deal more. What would we have done if we had had a chance like that? Well, this man took the land and paid the four hundred dollars. Two days afterwards he sold it for eight hundred dollars, but he did not pocket it all. He hunted his neighbor up and paid him extra on the deal. That man, you see, had a talk with God. Business is not merely a matter of results. It is a matter of exchange of values. That is the divine, right, God way of doing business, and this man let

God have his royal way in that transaction. His wife thought he was foolish, for she wanted another new dress, but he didn't feel foolish over his act. He felt that he had cleansed his way; and it was all a matter of thinking and coming to a correct judgment on his situation.

I do not care what your situation is, you have the great divine stirring within you, and if you let yourself think, you will ally yourself with what is right and come off more than conqueror. You can go with your emotions, your desires. When you do, you treat yourself badly and are ashamed of your conduct. You cannot dodge that better feeling of yours and be at peace with yourself.

Is that then what we mean by religion? What else can we mean? That is religion, vital religion, spiritual religion. It is a man doing business directly with God in the act of thinking, and getting at the truth and putting the truth to work. God is truth put to work. Whenever you put a piece of truth to work, you have established the Kingdom of God on earth; and there is such a stability about it. It is the way to build if we want to build in permanence.

I have been impressed this summer with the old Norman. I believe that he built along lines of truth, and that is why his architecture and his government have stood. William the Conqueror's old Domesday Book was a wonderful thing. William did some thinking there, and the result was the

Domesday Book that gave him a survey of his dominion and enabled him to govern intelligently. He has been falsely called the Conqueror. He was not a conqueror so much as a builder, and everything those Normans built was constructed along lines of thought, and therefore along lines of truth and stability. So much so that, after all the wars and rumors of wars, after all the wear and tear of the centuries, old England stands today with her face hopefully toward the future. With all her mistakes, she has tried to hew to the line, and in the main she has done so; and her leadership is still assured.

You come of that great race. America has all manner of other races upon her soil, but she has this great race of which I speak, and even with a Hearst syndicate against her, and all manner of emotional voices urging her away from the path of life, she stands committed in her Declaration of Independence and in her Constitution to the word of truth, to fair play in business, to decency in government, and to progress, to liberty, to civilization.

You have come here to learn about these things. You have come to study your life, not merely mathematics and history and the like. You have come to study citizenship and to fit yourself for the same.

See that you take yourselves seriously; that you learn to civilize your emotions; that you learn to think, and bring the power of reason to bear on all your problems; that, in other words, you ally yourselves with the word of God that was implanted in you at your birth; that you let come into your life the great, divine, perfect wisdom, the power of truth, that leaves you with a clear path before you, a sense of freedom and victory, a sense of satisfaction and joy in life.

I am not asking you this morning to do this or that, to study, to join the church, to be temperate, to be unselfish, to be good. I am simply asking you to give yourselves a chance so that you may realize who you are. You are a human being. As such you are a being with capacity to think and know the right, God thing to do. I am urging you, then, to let your rational part prevail, and I know that all the rest will follow. You will be a rational being; you will see your life in reason, and you will bring a sweet reasonableness to bear on all your transactions. In other words, you will be a Christian. For that, as I see it, is a Christian—a reasonable man or woman. I leave you with St. Paul's statement on this matter: "Present your bodies a living sacrifice, holy, acceptable unto God, which is your reasonable service." In other words: your bodies, the human body, is the seat of thought, emotions, and will. Then let your emotions come under the sway of the divine purpose within you. Let your emotions be ordered in reason, and you have it.

September 30, 1923

God is spirit; and they that worship him must worship him in spirit.—John 4:24.

NAMES are curious things. They used to have a heated discussion over this question: Is the name only a convenient and artificial term that we attach to an object, or does it set forth the nature of the object? For example, mule. Is the name "mule" only a hit-and-miss kind of thing, or does it in some way get at what the mule is? John McNeill, you remember, has a poem on the naming of the animals. An old darkey is puzzled over where the names came from and what they mean, and he finally comes to the conclusion that there is something in a name. "What's a bee?" he asks, "but just bee? And mule—what else could you call that animal with the long ears and black stripe down the back?"

There is insight in that poem. The old darkey had it right. Names are an attempt to get at reality; and they have a history. It takes a long time to find the right name for an object, and when it is found, it sticks. One of the essential things for a writer is to give his characters the right names, or to give his story—if it be a story—the right title.

The names we have given to God have passed through various stages, each representing a phase in the growing religious experience.

First he was thought of in terms of the Infinite. He was a solitary individual without any relation to life; and men worshiped him as such. They simply laid a sacrifice on the altar. There was nothing living in the transaction. There was nothing vital in religion then. It was a purely formal thing.

Then they began to think of God in terms of life. He became the living God. In what sense was he the living God? Where do we see the best expression of life? They said the best expression of life was the bull; and so they worshiped the bull, as the best expression of deity. In other words, the name of God at that stage was strength, force, energy—whatever word you wish to use. That called for a religion of power and a civilization based on power. Pyramids were the order of the day after they learned to think of God as strength.

A minister of religion had a discussion one day with Kipling. They were speaking of Cecil Rhodes, and the minister said that Cecil Rhodes was irreligious. "Irreligious?" asked Kipling. "Why, the man is building an empire." Kipling, in that discussion, was at the stage, religiously speaking, of power, strength.

And the name, power, given to God stands. God is strong, and efficiency is a chapter in religion.

Jesus discovered God as spirit. That is his contribution. And the conception of God as spirit has turned the tides of civilization. Our modern life—dating from the New Testament—has been growingly spiritual. It was not spiritual up to that time. It is not yet. But it is more spiritual than it was.

This, it would seem, is the final name for God. We cannot conceive of a more ultimate name. Spirit is universal. There is nothing limited in the word; and so we claim for our Christianity that it is the finished chapter of religion. If another man should discover a deeper, richer name for God, then Christianity would be superseded.

God is spirit. How connect with God? That calls for the spiritual in religion. God is spirit, and they that worship him must worship him in spirit. There is nothing else to do in the name of religion. A God who is spirit necessarily and naturally calls for a spiritual religion.

Let us look more closely at our subject and see how this is.

God is spirit. Spirit of what? For we must ask that question. Spirit is a very vague word until we get at its content. When we get at its content it becomes the most concrete and sensible and practical and rich word in the world.

God is spirit. The spirit of what?

For one thing, the spirit of truth; and one of the marks of a Christian is truth. You remember what our Lord said once: "For this cause came I into the world, that I should bear witness unto the truth." "The truth shall make you free."

The other day I heard two men talk of the late Joseph A. Holmes, who used to be our State Geologist. Dr. Holmes was one of the royal Christians, and he was such in respect of what these men said of him. He was absolutely free from prejudice. You could take any view of any matter you liked in his presence, and you would find him ready to look into your statement to see what of truth it contained. He had the power of orientation, as we call it, the capacity to go over to your side and see with your eyes.

That is one of the great marks of a Christian, and that is one of the noblest kinds of reverence—the spirit of truth in a man. "Is he a Christian?" we ask. He has an open mind, we say. That is Christianity in one of its royal chapters.

The other evening a stranger came into the car at Selma and sat beside me. We got talking of the railroads. "Mr. McAdoo," I said, "has stated that under government ownership the railroads made money. The stranger then paid his respects to Mr.

McAdoo. I am quite certain that much of what he said grew out of his political predilection. And in his libretto he did not give Mr. McAdoo all that was coming to him. His mind was prejudiced. In fact, his mind was biased on a lot of things. I gathered from his political libretto that he saw only one thing—that was the dear old Republican Party. Now, the Republican Party is old and dear to many people, and has rendered its unique service to civilization. But that does not necessarily save a man who is of that political persuasion from being prejudiced.

I found out from another stranger later that the Republicans never did anything right, and that we should draw a parenthesis around all those years that the Republicans have been in power.

I have heard Protestants say that we should put the Middle Ages and the Catholic Church in parenthesis—the Middle Ages and Catholic Church being a sort of ancient Republican Party, religiously speaking.

But that is to be partisan. God is spirit, the spirit of truth, and that calls for the spirit of truth in us, and when we have the spirit of truth, we are genuine children of God, genuine Christians to that extent. It is simple, is it not, but grand. I wish I could practice it. But I find myself with so many prejudices, even while I talk to you, that I am ashamed of myself. However, it is a glorious possibility of our life, and I am sure that more and more we are going to pre-empt the splendid region of the open mind. How did you work it out last week? Did you yield to your prejudices?

God is spirit. Spirit of what? Spirit of righteousness. That calls for the spirit of righteousness in us.

How are we to worship God? One of the real chapters of reverence is character. Whenever we do a good act we have proclaimed the presence and majesty of God in a way far beyond any hymns or prayers or swinging of incense. A good act—that is the real hymn, the real prayer, the real incense. "You can always trust him to do the right thing." When you can say that of a man, you have placed on him a genuine mark of Christianity.

Dean Stacy, who once guided the moral destiny of students in this institution, was a great Christian, and great in this respect—that his moral judgments were sound. He had in him the spirit of righteousness and knew always the right thing to be done. That was his contribution to this campus. The farther I travel from him, the larger his life looms up. He was a moral giant, and his very presence among us was redemptive along lines of conduct. Somehow, I never even saw him that I did not feel an elevation of character and the wonderfulness of being a man; and there are men all over this state today who not only remember Mr. Stacy with reverence, but who themselves would be ashamed to do a wrong deed simply because they knew him. In other words, he helped them to be Christian.

Duty, responsibility, service come in here. We are moral agents in our world. That means that we have certain exactions, responsibilities, laid upon us; and the man with the spirit of righteousness in him feels that he must shoulder his responsibilities. In other words, he feels that his life is a corporate as well as an individual thing, and he serves the cause of corporate well-being as much as his own immediate interests.

You gave to the cause of the Near East. Why? One of God's names is righteousness. Those Eastern people were in need, and the spirit of righteousness in you caused you to pay your debt to them. In that act you worshiped God along the line of conduct. You worshiped him in the beauty of Holiness. You were religious in the spirit of righteousness; and if any of us did not pay what we owed to those suffering folk, we were guilty of an impious act, no matter how fine or pious we may otherwise have been.

You hear people say: "What a lot of drives we are having. Will they never be done?" No, they will never be done. For we are living in a world that is an organism. We are all members one of another; and necessity is laid on us to have drives and to give. It is the right thing. It is our life and privilege as citizens in the world of God, whose name is righteousness. Service is not something tacked on to us. It is in our very nature as children of God and members one of another. And it is a chapter in Christianity.

Anything done right—from the running of a laundry, to the administering of a church—is God made real in life. It is God manifest in the flesh. It is Christ realized. It is the blessed story of the Incarnation repeated. God is spirit—the spirit of righteousness. Do the thing right, or better, have the spirit of righteousness, and in the spirit of righteousness, you cannot fail to do the thing right; and, as such, you are a reverent worshiper, not necessarily by the altar made with hands, but by the altar of responsibility.

Sometimes a young man here is very pious, but he loafs. The real piety is of the nature of work reverently and diligently and thoroughly done.

God is spirit. The spirit of what? The spirit of loveliness. That calls for the spirit of loveliness in us.

When I was at the East Carolina Teachers College, I went about through the various classrooms and into the infirmary and dining room and kitchen —everywhere. I did not find anything that was not pleasant, attractive to look upon. Every prospect was pleasing. The classrooms were attractive. The benches and walls were human and inviting. The dining room was administered much like a dining room in one of our homes.

There is a certain loveliness in nature, although nature is comparatively lacking on the side of beauty. She constantly needs the retouch of the hand of man. And what a difference between a scene of drab, prosaic aspect and one, for example, like that of our glorious hill country. There is all the difference there that we find between the man who does things in a slovenly manner and him who does what he does with finish.

The latter is what is sometimes called the artist in life. In the New Testament he is called the saint. "Called to be saints"—that is the way St. Paul expresses it.

In the Old Testament they were called to do the right thing. The law was the reality there. In the New Testament they are called to be saints. They have gone beyond law, righteousness. They have entered the blessed region of feeling. They have become artists, saints. Christ is the end of the law. The law is a schoolmaster to bring us to Christ. That means, I take it, that loveliness of life has to come in to crown our activity. Grace, that is the New Testament word. It is the man with the passion upon him not only to do the right thing but to do it in such a way that what he does is attractive.

Lots of good people are unattractive in their goodness. You can rely on them, but you do not love them. Their acts are so many straight lines. Jesus, it is said, was full of truth and righteousness too—yes, but full of grace. You had to love him. Going about in his world, he behaved so that people literally ran after him. He was the artist, the saint on the street.

He himself has a word about this: "Be ye perfect, even as your Father in heaven is perfect." By perfect he means more than righteous. He means being righteous in a lovely way.

John Calvin and John Knox were glorious men. History is indebted to them. They were great Christians as moral agents in their world. But they lacked the touch of art, the touch of sainthood. John Knox refused to take off his hat in the presence of his sovereign, the lovely Queen of the Scots. John Calvin was a fighter, and they needed fighters in that day. But Melanchthon had the loveliness. If John Calvin and John Knox had built a church!

Theodore Parker and Channing led the progressive religious movement of their day. They poured out their righteous souls in sermons and prayers and deeds that told mightily upon their day and subsequent days. Phillips Brooks had all that Channing and Theodore Parker had and then some. He added the touch of grace. The spirit of the altogether lovely was upon him; and the cause of Christianity had free course and was glorified in his hands.

What is the Lord telling us in all this today, in all this, his message of the spirit? Let us go back to his statement: "God is spirit, and they that worship him must worship him in spirit."

He is telling us, is he not, that we must live God. We have learned the formal approach to God. That is splendid. Form does enter into our life. But we must learn to live God. Then we have God always. He becomes an abiding presence. We generate him through our thinking, willing, and feeling. He sits enthroned in our hearts as truth and goodness and beauty.

Religion, according to the New Testament, is biological. It is the organic, vital relation of man and God. We literally breathe God. "Closer is He than breathing, and nearer than hands and feet." And that is spirituality. A spiritual being is not the pious being. Piety is the formal side of spirituality. A spiritual being is a life of freedom—a life free from prejudice, free from wrongdoing, and free from crudity. It is a life set free along the normally appointed lines on which the Christ's life moved.

A SERMON TO CHILDREN

WE ARE very much pleased to have you with us this morning and we hope that you will come here Sunday mornings and worship with the other people.

I hope you are to have—I was going to say I wished you a happy Christmas. But after all that would not be so much to say to you, would it? Just being happy. Well, I see practically nothing to that.

Boys and girls are apt to think that that is all there is to life, just being happy. And it means just having all the things you want and being rid of the things you do not want; having good clothes and money with which to buy gum and candy and toys and tickets to the moving picture place—all that sort of thing.

A lot of grown people think that way, too. They think that if they could have plenty of money and could travel and live in fine houses and go to the theatre and dance and so on, they would be happy and that would be all there was to life.

Well, a lot of people live that way, and the strange thing is that they are not even happy. If they were happy, that might be something, but people who live to be happy are not happy. Even if they were happy, they would be only like the animals. All that the animals want is happiness. The bears want a good coat of fur so that they will not feel the cold. And they want lots of berries on which they can feed. The sparrow wants only enough to eat and wants the other birds out of the way. It is strange, though, that when we have everything to make us happy we are not happy.

Why is this? Why are we not happy when we have everything to make us happy?

Well, there is more to life than things. Being a man, a real man, and being a real woman means more than just having all the things in the world. "How much is a man better than a sheep"—or any other animal!

Abraham Lincoln, for example, was born in a log cabin and was brought up not to have anything. He was glad, when he was a boy, if he could get enough grits and gravy for breakfast, to say nothing about dinner or supper. But I suppose you will agree that he was a real man. He began to be a real man while he was a boy. Instead of grouching around he worked and tried to do something for his home. And in the evenings, instead of grouching by the fireplace, he got hold of a book some one gave him and he read and improved his mind. Yes, and he forgot about his poverty in doing that. He was bigger than his poverty and was preparing to make something of himself in the world and help other people to make something of themselves. That is what I call being a man. And it is very much more important to be a man than merely to be happy. Suppose Abraham Lincoln had had everything he wanted and had become spoiled and had not become a real kind of man. Well, he would neither have been happy nor a man. The way to be happy is first to be a real man or woman. And every one of you can be a real man or woman.

Now, I have said all this in order to get you to think about what Christmas means. This week we are paying our homage. What is homage? We are paying tribute. What is tribute? We are praising a child who became not only a man but the greatest man the world has ever known. Who was he?

Jesus was the real kind of man. He was so great a man that he was called the "perfect man." And, remember, he was born poor. There are great men who were born rich. But most of us are born poor, and I want to show that being a man is the great thing, whether we are born poor or rich.

Jesus was born in a stable. There are no stables

now, only garages. Well, Mr. Strowd's garage would be a palace to be born in compared with the stable in which Jesus was born.

But he became a man. His father was a carpenter and he worked with his father at the carpenter's bench in Nazareth. He used to mend chairs and the like and carry them to the people who owned them. And all the time he was thinking about the importance of being a man, instead of thinking about whether he could get out of the carpenter's shop and go fishing. And he became a great man at last, and today we are worshiping him.

After he became a man, remembering the hard time through which he and his father and mother and brothers and sisters had come, he was always sympathetic with poor people. Yes, and he preached that everybody should try to live well, to have money and have comforts and pleasure. But he always taught that the important thing was to be a man, a woman. Here is the way he once put it: "I am come that ye might have life, and that ye might have it more abundantly." Having life means being men and women.

Now I am going to let you free. But I want first to say this to you: The way to be men and women —real men and women—is to be the best you can be wherever you are. That is what Jesus called loving and serving God. Loving and serving God is loving and serving the best.

You are here this morning and you are bored because the preacher is too long. But the real man or woman in you will be patient and try to find out what the preacher has to say.

You will be in school one of these days, and you will not be behaving, let us say, and you will be called to account by the teacher. The real man or woman in you then will say: "I deserved to be called to account." The unreal man or woman in you will go home to tell your parents about being badly treated by your teacher.

Tell the truth—that is being a real man or woman. Do what you are doing right, whether it is a sum in arithmetic, carrying in wood, or tying on your necktie, or going to Sunday School. Be on time, as we say, with what you are doing.

And there is something else. Take an interest in other people as well as in yourselves.

I saw a boy kick his dog the other day. A boy who is manly would not do that. But a boy who is not a man will do that. Boys sometimes love to tease their sisters or smaller boys. Well it is very human to want to tease other people. But you must be a man or a woman not to tease when you want to. Teasing is the way a cat treats a mouse. You do not want to be like a cat. And if you are bound to tease any one, I will say this to you—tease the boy that is bigger than you and take the results. There, at least, while you should not be teasing anyone, you have been man enough to face someone bigger than you.

Being a man—that means you are like Jesus. And that is what our Christmas is about. We are celebrating the name of the greatest man in the world. And the idea is not that we are to end with praising him, but that we are to be like him.

THE UNIQUENESS OF JESUS: A CHRISTMAS MESSAGE

God also hath highly exalted him, and given him a name which is above every name.
—Philippians 2:9.

History never makes a mistake in the names it places in its gallery of distinction. The cloud of criticism perpetually rising in their sky never successfully dims their splendor. Having lived, they remain enthroned in the human heart forever. And, having lived, they commit to succeeding ages the task of interpreting them. It is a serious task, for the precious gains of civilizations have their source, always, in the great man; and men interpret him in order that the civilizing process may, through him, be purified of its ancient obsessions and be thus further encouraged on its way.

Other men have emerged as bright particular stars in the firmament of history, to whom the world continually repairs for support. But in the foreground of this galaxy of spirits stands always the person of Jesus.

One of the biographers of Jesus declared that

God had given him a name that was above every name, and history has confirmed the statement. In our Western World this great spirit has drawn to himself the sustained devotion of nearly twenty centuries, while in the Orient he is being increasingly known and reverenced.

Hence our perennial return to a study of this central figure of our Western Hemisphere, a figure who is gradually pre-empting the homage of the world. While our Western life is not yet Christian, it is ideally such. With all our unfaith in theory and practice we desire both in public and private endeavor to attain to the excellence set forth in the Gospel story. And while, according to a modern interpreter of the Nazarene, he is the man whom nobody knows, he is the one man whom everybody hears about and should seek to appropriate in terms not only of reverence but of intelligence.

We have been giving him our reverence.

> "Through him the first fond prayers are said
> Our lips of childhood frame,
> The last low whispers of our dead
> Are burdened with his name."

But we may also see him intelligently. Christianity, in other words, is not an unenlightened enthusiasm. It is an experience that is grounded in reality, and this experience may be stated as genuinely in terms of thought and truth as the chemist states the case for the drop of water.

SERMONS

As we seek to wrest his secret from the man of historic splendor, our problem is to search for the unique element in his career that gave him his distinction. And such is our task as we apply ourselves to a study of him whom God has given the name that is above every name.

It has been affirmed that the superiority of Jesus lies in the supernatural origin claimed for him by his biographers. But similar origins have been claimed for other men. Besides, it is not how a man was born but what kind of a man he is that determines his status. He would be a courageous individual who repudiated the supernatural. When a man denies the supernatural, what he means is that he refuses to accept the supernatural in the form in which it has been presented to him. He is willing to grant, however, that all natural processes go back to that which is higher and other than himself. Hence the validity of the supernatural in the world. The difference, therefore, between objects is not the presence in one and the absence from the other of the supernatural, but the way in which they translate and illustrate their original endowment of reality. And Jesus Christ is to be tested not by his original endowment of reality but by his illustration of it in his daily life. To base his uniqueness on his origin is to set him forth in terms of that which is other than himself, not in terms of his achievement. And it is significant that he never refers to his origin as set forth by his biographers. He asks us to believe in him as divine but does so because he lived divinely, not because he had a divine origin. And two of his biographers, fascinated by the manner of his presence, make no reference whatever to his origin.

It is the fashion to say that the environment produces the man, and this has been a favorite explanation of the great man. But nothing is entirely made by its environment. The seed grows into a tree, relying on sun and air and soil, but there is something in the seed that assimilates the sun and air and soil and makes it possible, therefore, for its environment to work upon it. A dead seed never grows. Two men live in the same community at the same time. Why is it that one of them becomes a celebrity and the other remains in obscurity? The age in which Jesus was born was propitious. Civilization there and then was at the crossroads and in need of the great man to interpret and carry it forward. But why did he and not some other become the Saviour of the world? Why not John the Baptist or Pontius Pilate or the Caesar on the throne? But apart from this, to test a man by his environment is to interpret him in terms of that which is other than himself and not in terms of himself. And here we have a variation of the attempt to refer the uniqueness of Jesus to his origin.

One of the favorite explanations of the great man

is to say that he is the creation of his biographer. The human mind, it is affirmed, reads into the life it seeks to interpret much that is not there. A book has recently come from the press whose author seeks to show that the Man of Nazareth was wholly a creation of his biographers.

But there is always a man back of the story of a man, and there is always something in the man himself that stirs the imagination to accentuate his story. Else why has the biographer not seized on the name of Socrates or Plato or Philo or St. Paul and wrought it into the human consciousness as the name that is above every name?

The imagination applies itself to the great man, but the man is there first. The achievement of the imagination grows out of the man, never the man out of the achievement. And the achievement puts in its appearance as a complement to the man. The human mind is so enthralled by its subject that it feels it cannot treat it adequately without the aid of the shaping spirit of the imagination. And what the imagination contributes has virtue as well as the bare statement of fact. The story of the Cherry Tree is a touch of real biography. There is balm in tradition as well as in fact.

But to say that the great man is the product of his biographer is to center the interest in the biographer, not in the man. And that is another phase of the attempt to base the claims of Jesus on his origin or environment. It is to interpret him in terms of something foreign to him and not in terms of himself.

Reverent folk have always referred the superiority of Jesus to his miracles. But he made no such claim. They flocked around him with the passion for the miraculous, and he told them that their motive was a form of wickedness. "An evil and an adulterous generation seeketh after a sign." And recurrently in his ministry he not only refused to work miracles but expressed the wish that his followers would not base his claim on the miraculous.

Moreover, other men in other times have been associated with the miraculous. One was said to turn a rod into a snake and another to make an axe float in the water. In. India today the miracle worker is on every street corner and in every avenue and lane. And to claim for the uniqueness of Jesus his ability to work miracles is to place him in rivalry with others instead of stressing his originality.

The man who wrought miracles in the ancient world has emerged among us as the superman. But the world, applauding the superman, finds in him something to be feared rather than emulated. And if Jesus had based his claims on his exercise of superlative human power, he might have been another Alexander or Caesar, but not the superior being of the world.

The popular language applied to the great man

identifies him as a genius, and Jesus has been heralded as such. Our Emerson delights to mention him along with Plato or Socrates or Savonarola or some other whom humanity has honored as genius. The word genius, however, is like the surd in mathematics. And to speak of a man as a genius is to take refuge in a thought instrument, not in thought. But be this as it may, the impression formed from the word is that the man so labeled is of such marked ability that he stands apart from his fellows who can never hope even to emulate him. Genius is, therefore, another name for superman. But Jesus made no such claims for himself. "I am the Light of the World," he declares of his own person. And "Ye are the light of the world," he tells his followers, implying that they were potentially what he actually was. And his judgment passed on the miraculous power attributed to him is significant: "Greater works than these shall ye do."

In our study, therefore, of this great figure of history we find that there have been two attempts to set forth his uniqueness, the one centering in the supernatural, the other in the superman, the former presenting us with a divine but not a human being, the latter with only a human being, even if he is an enlarged illustration of human excellence. Papini, for example, stresses the divine nature of Jesus, while Mr. Bruce Barton stresses the human. Papini gives us the story of an emasculated being wearing a halo—the very being of all the beings in the world who had no interest in halos. Mr. Barton's "Man Whom Nobody Knows" is a superior administrator or a business expert like Mr. Barton. The biographies of Jesus, appearing from time to time, continue to interpret their subject in terms either of the divine or the human. In every instance we have a type of man presented to us but not the man in his totality, not the man in terms of himself.

Turning to the Gospel story we find the divine Jesus in St. Matthew and St. Luke, the man of action and power in St. Mark; while in St. John the biographical interest moves on another plane. According to the latter's statement, Jesus Christ stands in history as the first man who saw the essential unity of God's world and man's world, who saw the world as the living presence of Reality, of which the human being was the finished expression, and who lived for the real and divine and enduring things because it was his nature to do so. He was, therefore, the first man to believe in himself and express himself and live and grow and find his freedom. And this means that the individual emerged for the first time in Jesus of Nazareth. He believed in and expressed himself because he found in his experience those permanent values on which he could rely. And in all the relations in which he stood he released the values that were seeking expression in his experience, thus giving to the details of his life a touch of splendor and to his fellows the spectacle of a man in all the full, rich beauty of manhood.

Here we come on the spectacle of a man in his totality, what Jesus calls the perfect man and St. Paul the saint—a man, not with a halo about his brow, but with all his capacities of thought and will and feeling in bloom. The reason why Raphael painted a picture that has a name above every name in pictorial art is that he left nothing out of his enterprise and achievement. There was a perfect blending of the artistic elements in that sublime creation. Mr. Ty Cobb has enjoyed a name above every name in the realm of athletics because the perfect man, athletically speaking, the man in the happy co-ordination of brain and hand and heart, was realized in him. Enlarge the thought from art and athletics to living, and in the Man of Nazareth we have the perfect man on the street, in the home, in the presence of all manner of people and relations. He was a man, here among men, associated with the problems, and cares, and perplexities of the common day. But he never sounded a retreat from life nor ever by a mere masterful exercise of his will compelled his environment to do his bidding. Instead, patiently and gently but surely he brought to every detail of his experience the serene white light of love and thought and action. He knew the thing to be said and done and did it with the unerring touch of fine feeling that gives enlargement to knowledge and tempers action with justice and beauty.

And this perfect man saw the capacity for perfection in his fellow beings and encouraged them to believe in themselves and express themselves and live and grow and find their freedom. "Be ye perfect," he said to them, and he meant that. He encouraged them because he saw the possibility that was throbbing within them and that only needed encouragement to express itself. Jesus and his disciples present us with the spectacle of a group of men who "gave a welcome to all those things both higher and lower that have a right to enter a man's life and dominate it." This is the story of what has been technically called the Incarnation—the divine and permanent in man, and man seeking and finding the divine and permanent within him.

The whole biography of man centers in the attempt to effect a unity between him and the divine. Early in his career he became aware of the finite and changing nature of his human world. He found that everything he touched eluded his grasp. The sun rose and also set. He made his plans that miscarried. The spectacle of finiteness and change confronted and appalled the early man as it confronts and appalls the modern man.

He found that there was something in his world

that was interfering with and interrupting the apparent order, something that was higher than and superior to himself. That higher and superior power he called God. And his problem, henceforth, lay in the attempt to relate himself to God, to find the divine and thus find his security and peace in a changing world. But the ancient man failed to effect the relation. He found the divine but lost the human. He discovered God but located him in another world. And his only hope lay in turning his face from his human world, in which, despite its transitory nature, he continued to be interested. Yes, and failing at length to appropriate the divine, he turned again to the world to be unhappy there.

Greek culture came in as one of the grand but futile efforts to relate the human and divine. It was a brave venture of the human spirit that has value still. Great men figured there whose names have become household words, none of which, however, has become the name that is above every name.

The Greek started with a vivid sense of his environment. He was a child of the material order. But he was a thinking spirit who, in his analysis of things seen and temporal, discovered the things unseen and eternal, the things of God, the things, namely, that are enduring and divine. His discovery he called the ideal country. God, for him, became identified with the ideal. But in his pursuit of this ideal, permanent, divine world he lost touch with the world of human affairs. The finished contribution of that ancient chapter of culture was Plato's Republic, and it was an ideal state, not a state on the map. The best Plato could do was to suggest the creation of a cultured and leisure class who found release from the world of human affairs by despising it. The Greek failed to see that culture was not only of the Acropolis and the Apollo Belvedere, but of the market place, the home, the street, and all the commonplace relations in which men stand. There was no hope for man as such in that program of civilization. And men faced their cares and performed their tasks as if Plato and his Academy had never existed, pretty much as they do today surrounded by the educational institutions they pay taxes to support. In other words, the Greek caught sight of the divine but never realized the divine in life. Supermen emerged then like Plato and Aristotle and Demosthenes, but not men clothed in the splendor of daily living after the manner of the Man of Nazareth.

The Roman Empire was another grand but belated attempt to relate the human and divine. The founders of the Empire claimed for it a divine origin. The great man emerged there, who, receiving his commission from God, built the Empire and became its sovereign. His sovereign power was delegated to him from God and carried with it divine honors. In the days of Jesus the Empire prevailed everywhere, and men declared with pride that they were Roman citizens. But Rome with all her social cohesion was languishing when Jesus lived. It failed to be the tree whose leaves were for the healing of the gap between man's world and God's world. And it failed because it, too, sounded a retreat from life. It reckoned without the individual. Private interests were absorbed and lost in the social system. Men saw no connection between their private concerns and the public interests, and many of them, being slaves, were supposed to have no private concerns. The Roman people had their Forum but not the thought of the personal righteousness that exalteth a nation. Glorious monuments were raised in memory of heroic men, but the heroes in the daily battle of life had no significance. Vast wealth was spent on public buildings and places of amusement, but nothing in the attempt to create better opportunity for the individual man.

The Roman discovered the world of God but lost the world of man. Supermen emerged there who impressed their power on citizens and slaves, but the gap remained between men and their personal heritage in the things that count and abide.

The Jew worshiped Jehovah, an infinite being of righteousness who had selected the Prophet to write and commit his laws to the people for their observance. But the program failed to effect the unity between man and the divine because it also sounded a retreat from life. It pointed to the Temple but never attempted to bring the Temple to the home and vineyards and sheepfolds. The story of the talk between Jesus and the woman of Samaria who asked him about the correct place in which to worship is significant here. Judaism was entirely removed from the private life of the Jew. Supermen emerged there in the persons of the Scribe and Priest and Prophet, but the rank and file of the people, while reverencing these supermen, were as the hungry sheep that look up and are not fed.

With all the failure, however, of the ancient people, let it be repeated that they made a grand contribution to civilization. They discovered God. In other words, they discovered their inheritance in the permanent and divine and ideal. Their failure lay in their inability to translate the permanent and divine and ideal into daily living. Discovering God, they were never able to put him to work in their daily affairs and relations. They worshiped him but they failed to experience him and practice him. Ancient civilization never thrilled the lives of men as men.

Yes, and when Jesus made his advent he came upon a state of bankruptcy. The human being knew that to live truly and blessedly he should live divinely. But, failing to attain the divine, he found himself in skepticism and despair and was utterly weary with his life in the world. Greek civilization had been absorbed by Rome, and its culture had ended in cynicism. The Roman Empire was writing its own epitaph, and even the citizens, to say nothing of the slaves, were hopeless. Judea was not only under the dominion of Rome, but the younger generation there had turned its back on the law and the prophets.

These all had sighted the Ideal Country as Columbus sighted America. The development of America, however, passed to other hands. And the development of the Ideal Country passed into the hands of him who, in his own language, came to establish the Kingdom of God upon earth.

The situation that prevailed at the time of Jesus was similar to that with which we are confronted today. The school—the sequel to Plato's Academy—is busy with its program of culture which makes for wisdom but not necessarily for the wise life. The state—the sequel to the Roman Empire—is making laws and thus filling social prescriptions for the individual but not necessarily diagnosing his disease. The church—the sequel to the ancient Temple—is administering ecclesiastical but not necessarily personal religion. Jesus met that situation in the peculiar form in which it confronted him, and in calling him the Saviour of the world we mean that by his profound insight, for which he forfeited his life, he enabled civilization to go forward. He founded and administered a school and was thus a friend of culture. But the men he taught went into the world with truth made alive in their experience. "I am the truth," he said. And again: "If the truth shall make you free you shall be free indeed." Mere knowledge to Jesus was but the veneer of culture. He taught the truth of religion, and in teaching it he aroused in his pupils the passion to put it to work in the world. And he would say that the teaching of any subject was futile if it had not a similar result. Truth for truth's sake and not for humanity's sake he would consider a pleasant pastime but not the end of real culture.

He founded and administered a state, but it was a state in which all were for each as well as each for all. He founded and administered a church, but religion to him was first a personal experience. He taught that God was Spirit and that men first found him in their hearts, then built their church. He thus gave to the divine and ideal a local habitation and name. He made God a force in life. Beginning with men, he opened wide to them the gates of life and possibility and faith and hope. He proclaimed the ideal to men by presenting them with the spectacle of the man with ideals. He proclaimed God to men by the spectacle of the Godman. Instead of heralding the divine and claiming divine honors, he stood before men as the divine man and claimed for every man the power to express the divine where he was and in what he was doing and enjoying and suffering. The human and divine, he declared, were a unit. "I and my Father are one." And "I come that ye may find your life on its divine and therefore abundant side." "The Son of Man" he called himself. But by a Son of Man he meant a Son of God. Look long enough at a Son of Man and in him you are obliged to find God. And the place, pre-eminently, to find God, is in Man. "The Kingdom of God is within you." The human being is the de luxe edition of life, and as such he is the finished illustration of the great creative Spirit in whom all things live and move and have their being.

And, thrilled by his teaching and person, men flocked around him from all the various walks of life. The reverent Jew, dissatisfied with his ecclesiasticism, turned to him. Roman citizens and slaves, wearied with their social system, became his converts. Greek culture sought him out and finally lent its language for the writing of his biography. There was a tremendous stirring of lives everywhere, the net result of which was the formation of the Christian society within the Empire, in which men found their unity with the divine and their unity, therefore, with each other. It was a divine-human society in which the Greek and Roman and Jewish attempts at civilization were fused in what has blossomed as our modern Democracy with its School and State and Church.

But the modern school is very different in its aim from the school as administered by Plato—thanks to the advent of Jesus. It is very different in aim although not always in practice, for still the old Platonic idea of culture that is away from life prevails. Matthew Arnold took the Cornell institution to task for its attempt to relate culture to commerce. He was a British Plato, who failed to see that culture is the harmonious development of the individual. The apostles of this ancient culture are still in evidence, but they are belated heralds of education. For on the soil of America we are committed to the program of culture that is a coming to know that we may be better able to live. Here on this soil, committed to the cause of the individual, we are coming to see that the culture of the hand is as glorious as the culture of the brain. We believe that every form of work—work in the mill and mine and home and market place and on the street—is a medium through which the spirit of man may attain its perfection and freedom. And the latest cultural movement among us is adult education, the bringing of the program of the school to men where they are amidst the grime and smoke and wear and tear of toil and business.

The modern state has a very different aim from that of the Roman Empire—thanks to the advent of Jesus. Centralized government prevailed in that ancient system, and the individual was a cog in the machine. But once when Jesus was asked to solve the problem of taxes, he replied: "Render unto Caesar the things that are Caesar's and unto God the things that are God's," the implication of his reply being that a man stands both in the image of God and as a member of the social order; yes, and being in the image of God he is first a man and afterwards a social being, and the social order that reckons without the consent of the human beings that constitute it is like the body that would reckon without limbs or arms. We are committed to a government that is in the interests of men. Citizenship was purchased under the ancient rule. A man is born a citizen among us and, coming of age, is expected to take a personal interest in the civic welfare and make a contribution, however small, to the civic venture. American civilization is every American's privilege and responsibility.

There are apostles of civilization among us who, harking back to the ancient method, stand as champions not of the rights of men but of the rights of a special class. Industry has its champions. Business has its champions. The farmer has his champions; as if any man or class of men constituted the state! It is significant, however, that every varied interest is being championed even if the champions are sectarian in their devotion. And, gradually, in our crude and dull manner we are working out on this soil a social order in which every claimant shall have his dues, banker, merchant, capitalist, toiler, farmer, the man on salary, and the man of money and privilege.

Religion today has a very different aim from that of the Pharisaic system—thanks to the advent of Jesus. In the hands of the Pharisee religion was mathematicized, and the people were supposed to bow reverently to the religious formula. But we are gradually absorbing the teaching of Jesus that religion is a personal experience and therefore the light of the world and not merely a formula. There are apostles of Jesus, today, who, reverting to the Pharisaic method, would deny to men their ancient right to think and would saddle upon them a form of belief, who are saying that the world is a wicked place and are setting up a gap between secular and sacred. But the thought of Jesus is quietly making its way among us that the world is good in the making, that men are essentially religious, and that, engaged in their secular pursuits with clean hands and pure hearts, they are spreading the Kingdom of God on the earth.

Ancient civilization was founded on the principle that a man could do nothing right and was therefore in need of a guardian. The guardian emerged as the man of culture who arrogated to himself the responsibility of warding off catastrophe. The guardian emerged as the head of the social system who worked out the formula for social cohesion. The guardian emerged as the Priest or Scribe or Prophet who also sought to whip the fumbling and stumbling human being into line. Modern civilization, smugly professing to be Christian, has been repeating the sins of the ancients. We are still at the stage of the formula and guardian. And the net result of our civilizing process is like what happens when the hen leads her ducklings to the bank of the stream. The formula and guardianship are of no avail. Everybody is getting out from under, and it is a case of the Devil take the hindmost.

According to Jesus men are born to go right as the sparks to fly upward, and, given a chance, they will, God helping them, work out their own salvation. And the story of Jesus is a parable of life. It is a parable of every child born into the world— every infant in the mother's arms a young Messiah to be nurtured as a precious unit of life that is eventually to radiate life and light in the world! The story of Jesus is a parable of the rebirth of civilization out of its ignorance, out of its vice and slums and squalor, out of its poverty and crime, its weariness and fever and fret, into the light that is never extinguished and the beauty that is uncreated —into the Kingdom of God upon earth.

The spirit of reverence in man, making many a mistake, has been forever toiling upward in its search. And, as men lift their voices in prayer and praise to the Man of Nazareth, their reverence touches hands with one who turned the tides of history and therefore merits the name that is above every name.

CHRISTIANITY AND ROMANTICISM

And the Word was made flesh, and dwelt among us, (and we beheld his glory, the glory as of the only begotten of the Father,) full of grace and truth.—John 1:14.

IN THIS STATEMENT we have a summing up of that wonderful little document known as the prologue to the Gospel of St. John.

In the first sentence of that prologue the author tells us what he means by "the Word": "In the beginning was the Word, and the Word was with God, and the Word was God." The prologue is an account of the creation of the world, and he thinks of creation as a growth out of the life of God. It is the nature of any living thing to expand. In God, St. John declares, was life, and his life, parting from itself, unfolded into the world as a seed into a plant, or a mother's life into a child's life. The world, therefore, according to this great New Testament document, was a birth. It is God's child. As such it has been not an addition of one thing to another, or an addition of the whole to the being of God, but a multiplication and revelation of the indwelling life of the Creator. And, as the child bears the lineage of its parentage, the world, in the large and in the small, is by nature divine. God has repeated himself in every fragment of creation. The world is therefore a unity, not a dualism. We are to think not of God and the world, but of God in the world. The poet has it right:

"I doubt not thro' the ages one increasing purpose runs,
And the thoughts of men are widened with the process of the suns."

All the various states of the world are, therefore, bound together as a commonwealth. A federal life pervades the whole. The world is a unity in all its vast variety. Nothing walks with aimless feet. "All things are of God," as the great Apostle expresses it. Our world with all its color and form is therefore not only beautiful to behold, but it is beautiful because it unfolds the divine idea. It is not only a playground, but a sacred and serious place. Every appeal of beauty is sacramental and, therefore, a call to reverence. The world, as Goethe has described it, is the living, visible presence of God.

The creative process finally took the form of man and reached its climax in the perfect man, Christ Jesus. In him God became flesh, and dwelt among us, full of grace and truth.

The prologue of the Gospel of St. John is an account of creation similar to that of the first chapter of Genesis, with this exception: In the first chapter of Genesis the creative process ends with man, while in St. John's Gospel it ends with the perfect man. "We beheld his glory"—his distinction, the glory, the distinction—"as of the only begotten of the Father, full of grace and truth." The perfect man! The man, namely, whose life is an exact image, a repetition, of the life of God.

"Yes," you say, "I have been hearing all my life this story of the divinity of Christ, but it has always seemed to me so general and vague that I have never been able to take it seriously." Let us, then, listen to St. John as he unfolds the story of the divinity of Christ: "We beheld his glory, the glory as of the only begotten of the Father, full of grace and truth." Such is his statement of what he means by the perfect man, the divine man, the man in the exact image of God.

Grace is beauty. And in saying that Jesus was full of grace, the writer means that he was a lover and seeker of the things that make for pleasure, happiness, satisfaction, joy—all those things that come within the sweep of beauty. In other words, the spirit of romance and venture was upon him. He was a champion of the state rights of experience.

But such is only the form of beauty. With the spirit of romance and venture upon him, he sustained the spirit of reverence. A lover and seeker of beauty, he felt the seriousness of life, and had his earthly joy always touched by and in control of the divine joy. "Wist ye not," he declared when a boy, "that I must be about my Father's business." That program of life announced in youth became the program of his later years.

St. John's way of stating this attitude of Jesus is that he whose life is full of beauty is also full of truth. Romance, in him, was the servant of reality. He sought nothing that was not in keeping with the divine purpose that rules the world.

Everything of beauty is an illustration of something, some idea, some unit of value, some reality, some purpose, that under the hand of God has unfolded into that particular thing—the divine idea of the mother's love, for example, that has unfolded itself into the form and color of Raphael's great picture; the divine principle of H_2O that has unfolded itself into the dew-drop; the divine and mystic principle of vegetation that has unfolded itself into the flower.

The genuine lover and seeker of beauty is one who looks for the truth, for the unit of value, for the purpose, for the reality, in every lovely appeal that comes in on human life. You are familiar with the ode by young Keats on the Grecian urn. That fragment of beauty and joy to him was a perfect specimen of its kind. Looking upon it, he felt that it embodied the principle not only of art but of life, and addressing that ancient form of loveliness, he wrote:

"When old age shall this generation waste,
   Thou shalt remain, in midst of other woe
Than ours, a friend to man, to whom thou say'st,
'Beauty is truth, truth beauty,'—that is all
   Ye know on earth, and all ye need to know."

But a human life illustrates this principle of perfection better than a fragment of art. And the glory of Jesus was that, full of beauty, he was full of truth. A lover and seeker of life on its side of form and color and pleasure, he kept covenant with the high and enduring things of God. Thrilled with the spirit of romance and venture, he was also thrilled with the spirit of reverence and restraint. With his life of beauty thus unified with God's good purpose, he stands as the perfect man, the man in God's image, and the climax of creation—yes, and the supreme illustration of what we are by nature, and may become in fact. I never read any little fragment of the gospel story that I do not see a parable of my own life.

Our life moves in the region of beauty. We are in a world of form and color and sound that appeals to us in myriads of ways. Yes, but in and through these myriads of appeals to our human sense is the great divine appeal of reality. And when we learn to have our sense of joy tempered by the sense of reality, we have learned to live the full, free, abundant life of a man.

I used to have the idea that to be a Christian

meant to live a somber kind of life, removed from the world. I felt that it must be a wicked thing to indulge in any enjoyment, and that the fewer enjoyments a man had, the bigger Christian he was and the larger hope he had of heaven at last. But the world is not a wicked place. All good things are ours, and all things are good in the making. They are all the living embodiment of the one grand joy of God, and allied with the thought of what God wants us to be and do; no enjoyment of our world can ever do us harm.

The harm comes in when we enjoy in the trivial mood that seeks merely to enjoy. It is the romantic nature in man that, restive under authority and restraint, turns the seeking of beauty into a bestial thing. The prodigal in his early career was a romanticist who ended in the bestial manner. He was full of grace but not of truth, a seeker of beauty but not of reality and stability. There was no unified power in his life. He was as the ship without chart and compasses, the farmer without any consistent idea of agriculture, the business man who relies on the tricks of the trade instead of on his intelligence.

The Pharisee, who administered religion when Jesus lived, had the somber idea of religion. He was a stranger and pilgrim in his world. He presents us, therefore, with the classical chapter of life that finds no place for freedom and enjoyment.

Beauty was cast forth from his program of living as an orphan child. The classical spirit and the romantic spirit met in the person of Jesus. He held to the jots and tittles of the law, while arrogating to himself the privilege of the world of beauty. The classical people, in the persons of the Pharisees, failing to understand his love of beauty, turned against him; and the romanticists, in the persons of the Sadducees, failing to understand his love of law and order, also turned against him. At last the climax came when Pilate exclaimed: "What will you do with Jesus, who is called the Christ?" They took him and crucified him. But the question still stands: "What will you do with Jesus, who is called the Christ?" Failing to take him seriously and be saved by his passion for beauty tempered by restraint, we also can crucify him. But, like the disciples of old who saw in him a parable of their life, we may read the parable they read, and, inspired by its teaching, with the spirit of grace and truth, we may become partakers of their achievement of perfection. The story of Jesus is an illustration in every detail of this perfect life of beauty and truth.

I remember a little chapter of unwritten biography that a woman once illustrated in a community where I was privileged to live. Her life, when I first came to the community, was full of grace but not of truth. She was a lover and seeker of her world on its side of joy but had no seriousness in her romantic venture. She declared she had no interest in the church or religion, and all her time was spent in social pleasures. One day, however, a community club was started in that place, in which some of her friends became interested, and within twenty-four hours her heart turned in that direction. She had been enjoying the fair things in her community without seeing the real and enduring things that were there. She had given herself to the social whirl without feeling the still, sad music of the human beings about her whose lives were on the treadmill. But her hour of inspiration and transformation came, and her life, hitherto full of beauty, became full of truth. She cast in her influence with those who in that community club began to think of human welfare as well as of their personal enjoyment. She became interested in the young people about her who had no mooring in their homes and who were spending their evenings in the pleasure-seeking that kills. She became interested in the church and found a joy she had formerly missed in its opportunity of worship and service. And in these and many other ways she finally stood as an illustration of what St. Paul wrote to the Roman Christions: "Be not conformed to this world, but be ye transformed by the renewing of your mind, that ye may prove what is that good, and acceptable, and perfect will of God." Or better still, she stood in that community as an illustration of the perfect life set forth in the words of St. John, applied to Jesus, "We beheld his glory, the glory as of the only begotten of the Father, full of grace and truth."

Are there any individuals in Chapel Hill who stand in need of this transformation and renewal of life? I hope there are not, but if there are, they are making a cheap use of life, and I hope they will find the renewal.

One day when Jesus was in Jerusalem he found a crippled man downstreet who, in company with other wretched folk, was languishing by an ancient pool that was supposed to have healing value for those who could make use of its opportunity. Jesus stopped on his way and talked with the man and healed him of his malady. Later, he found this man in the temple and said something to him there that was significant. "Sin no more," he said to him, "lest a worse thing befall thee."

That man was healed not merely in body but in mind. He had been a lover and seeker of beauty but not of truth. His life, full of grace, had been empty of reality. He had been a sower to the wind— yes, and had reaped the whirlwind, a sower to the flesh, and a reaper of corruption. But through the personal, benign touch of the Man of Nazareth he learned to sow to the spirit and to reap life and freedom and peace.

Many a young man has repeated the romantic venture of that ancient man and cripple. He has sought beauty but not truth. He has given his heart to joy but not reality. And the healing pools are full of these crippled folk, seeking a return of the reality of health they have squandered, and sad over their moral failure. We all hark back to Lord Byron's description of this physical and moral collapse:

> "My days are in the yellow leaf;
>   The flowers and fruits of love are gone;
> The worm, the canker, and the grief
>   Are mine alone!"

"A young man," it is said, "is obliged to sow his wild oats." No. He is obliged to sow wheat or corn or some similar variety of life in the soil of his experience. He can sow the wild variety, but it is forever a mistake. Fair and prosperous looking at first, a little way above the soil it gives sign of a malignant presence. Blessed is the youth who, stirred with the sense of beauty that invites to licentiousness, has felt the stirring of the deeper sense of truth that invites to restraint. One of the wonderful things said by Jesus—and that would be a splendid motto with which to adorn the room of a dormitory—is that fragment which has become familliar from the Sermon on the Mount: "Blessed are the pure in heart; they see God." And the man who, in his love of beauty, acts on that high principle of Jesus enters in that experience into a compact with the perfect life that is full of grace and truth.

One day as Jesus was teaching, a man suddenly ran up to him and said: "What good thing shall I do to inherit eternal life?" He was a man of culture and wealth and position and lineage. And he was full of grace, full of the sense of beauty that goes with wealth or position or lineage. But his life was empty of truth. Nobody at home. No real downright reality in his heart. He had a serious side to his nature, but not so serious that it had found its freedom in human understanding. He had been paying a sort of courteous deference to the true way of living, but that was all. And Jesus said to him: "Sell that thou hast, and give to the poor, and thou shalt have treasure in heaven; and come, follow me." Appealing to that man as a man of position and wealth and lineage, he pressed upon him the claims of truth, of reality. "You are a man of position. Why not use your position in a serious instead of a trifling manner? You have wealth. Why spend it all on yourself, without a thought of the responsibility it carries? You have lineage. Why be a snob, when you can be a human being and show your identity with the people who do not enjoy your social privilege?" Position, with the power it involves, is a splendid thing. Let us have power.

But true power is a thing to be not only enjoyed but shared. "All power is given unto me," said Jesus, "in heaven and in earth"; and then: "Go ye into all the world, and preach my gospel to every creature." He could have had his power for himself, but he used it to make the world a better and happier place. He was of the royal house of David, but see how he commingled with the fisher folk and all the crude and unlettered people around him, making them feel that the rank is but the guinea stamp, and a man is a man irrespective of his rank. He had no money, but he felt that he had rather be poor than rich and a Sybarite like the rich young ruler. "What good thing shall I do to inherit eternal life?" The man who asked that was as a fraternity man on a campus, and Jesus said, "Fine; but don't stop there. Be a fraternity man, enjoying its beauty, but make it your business as a fraternity man to relate your privilege in some real and vital manner every day to your fellow man." The man who asked the question was as a man on a campus with plenty of money at his disposal, and Jesus said: "Splendid, but how are you spending your money? On week-ends and moving pictures and other appeals of the world of joy, without a thought of how you might use it to aid some self-help man?" The man who asked that question was as a man on a campus in the heyday of success, and Jesus said to him: "I congratulate you on your success, but why let it run to your head? Blessed are the poor in spirit, for theirs is the kingdom of heaven."

I have been talking to you today about the supreme and sublime fact of the world. It is the fact we know as the Incarnation—God in human limbs arrayed. This is the precious truth of the Shekinah, the glory of the divine presence in the world that moved the ancient Jew to a sense of wonder and awe. First, the Jews thought of God as present in the storm. Then the ark, containing his essence, became their sacred symbol. Later, they thought of him as dwelling in the holy of holies in the temple, and finally the law became identified with his glory. In Jesus Christ God became incarnate in man. There is something to stir our sense of awe and reverence in the thought of Jesus Christ—the living presence of God in the world, functioning as a citizen in the Kingdom of God, as the arm functions as a part of the body; not a preacher about God, but a God-intoxicated man; not merely a religious worker, but a man with an exalted religious experience; not merely a theologian, but a man whose thought and will and feeling were saturated with the mind of God. No wonder they felt the sublimity of his life and bowed in reverence before it. And the glory of this man of grace and truth is that he is a parable of your life and mine. We, too, can bring God to pass on our streets, in our homes, and our daily activities. We, too, living among men, can have them say of us: "We beheld his glory, the glory as of the only begotten of the Father, full of grace and truth."

Have I helped you to see the face of God today?

If I have not, I have utterly failed. For the business of the preacher is not to entertain his audience, but to show God to them. The day is passing when the preacher shall find it necessary to say smart things in the pulpit and try to win through tricks of thought and speech. Men are by nature divine and are looking for God. And God help us all to find him.

Love never faileth.—I Corinthians 13:8.

This is the first Sunday in the New Year, and I want to try to say something appropriate to the season. Quietly, silently, the old year left us, and we are now writing our letters under the date 1924. It was about this month, 1904, that I came to Chapel Hill, and it is startling to me to reflect that I have been identified with this dear old place nearly twenty years. When we say that time flies, we speak in absolutely accurate language.

And what changes have taken place in those twenty years! North Carolina has grown into a new state. Chapel Hill has become a new place. Old things have passed away. All things have become new. The hand of change is upon everything. It is upon our own lives, and our great problem is how to handle this fact of change.

We are in a changing world. Is there anything in this changing world that remains permanent?

Can we rise above the change? Can we seize upon anything that remains steadfast?

St. Paul says there is one thing that abides. He calls it love. Men have tried everything else and found themselves disappointed. Wherever they have tried love, they have never been disappointed.

What does he mean by love? He describes it, "Love suffereth long, and is kind; love envieth not; love vaunteth not itself, is not puffed up, doth not behave itself unseemly, seeketh not her own, is not easily provoked, thinketh no evil; rejoiceth not in iniquity, but rejoiceth in the truth; beareth all things, believeth all things, hopeth all things, endureth all things. Love never faileth."

In other words, love is feeling. It is a feeling for what is true and right and fair. When a man rises into that high place of living, he has risen above the change, and even in his world of shifting base he remains steadfast. For he is rooted in that which refuses to change.

Take any change you please. Today, the lines are fallen unto you in pleasant places. But tomorrow, the bludgeonings of chance or circumstance get in their work. Every one of us has that experience. You young people have not had much of that yet. Everything has gone pretty well with you. But as you go on, you will come upon such hard experiences. The rosy morn of youth will pass into the drab day of clouds. How are you going to maintain the buoyancy of youth when you look upon that drab day of clouds?

Love is the secret here. Love suffereth long, and still remains the kindly thing it is. If you meet your suffering in the spirit not of bitterness but of gentleness and patience, and with an understanding heart, you will hold your own through suffering.

A great many people go to pieces under the stress and strain of untoward circumstance. They grow embittered and despondent. But when the understanding heart prevails, the circumstance is handled beautifully, and the better man emerges from the pain.

I think of a friend who once held a prominent position in which he suffered from a thankless public. He had enough piled on him to submerge his life, but all the way along he kept his head, he remained gentle and patient and forgiving. In other words, he handled the situation in which he found himself, and without one feeling of bitterness in his heart he shouldered his responsibility and did his work faithfully to the last. That man stands, today, after all the bludgeonings of the years, satisfied with life, having found something to tie to that remained fixed while everything else changed. Criticism? Why, yes. But he took the criticism not in antagonistic but in receptive mood, and went beyond it. He still cherished his fellow beings who did the criticizing, and after the shafts of scorn and meanness were spent, he remained intact. Nothing can put the man down who has love in his heart like that.

Take this other chapter of change. You see other people succeed around you, and are aware of your own failure as compared with them. It is difficult for us to maintain our status when we try hard and fail, and when at the same time we see others about us who have succeeded and did not try as hard, perhaps, as we. But if love comes to our rescue here, we maintain our status. And love, in this sentence, is described by the Apostle in these terms: "Love envieth not."

When we get into the royal way of living that leaves us delighted with the success of others, even when we ourselves fail, we have risen above our failure. The real failure, here, is envy. The real success is the power to rejoice with those who rejoice.

One of the grand things on this campus is the way the contestants for honors and positions and prizes regard each other. They do their best to win, but when they fail, they congratulate their neighbors who have beaten them. I had rather have that kind of success than the greatest honor, the highest position, the most cherished prize, and not be capable of rising above the spirit of envy. For there I have something that is steadfast. I have one of those timeless things of the spirit. I have love, and such love never fails.

Dr. Meyer preached at one time to crowded houses in London City. He held the loyalty of thousands of human beings in his heart. One day Campbell Morgan began to preach in a church across the way, and the people who once flocked to Dr. Meyer now flocked to Campbell Morgan. It was a stern experience for the old preacher, but he rose above it. "I am grateful for the overflow from Dr. Morgan's church," he said. In that rare feeling he found himself rejoicing in the other man's success, and he himself remained steadfast before the spectacle of his waning power. It was love that never faileth.

Take another chapter in the story of change. Sometimes a man is caught and whirled about in the maelstrom of success. A lot of people go to pieces here. They rise to social prominence, or to power of one kind or another, and then the danger comes and conceit gets in its work. How are we to stand firm amidst our successes? It is more difficult to bear success than failure.

Jesus thought of this once when he was preaching. There were some successful people in his audience. Perhaps they were rich. Perhaps they were being socially lionized. And he uttered these sublime words: "Blessed are the poor in spirit, for theirs is the Kingdom of Heaven." It is the only way to stand success—humility of spirit, the fine feeling that sees in success a chance, not to become conceited, but to serve. It is love again getting in its good work.

St. Paul speaks of this very thing. "Love is not puffed up." Where love is, a man can have any success and maintain himself wonderfully in the experience. Where love is not, success will ruin the best kind of man.

I have seen young men rise into success on this campus and become so conceited that they were unbearable. Usually it goes the other way. When they find themselves borne on the crest of the wave, they are then most reverent and beautiful in their lives. They have something deeper in their lives than success. They have love, and love keeps them from being selfish and brutal. It keeps them intact.

There is another chapter of change. It is when a man comes to the place where he has a chance to make a fool of himself. Have any of you made fools of yourselves lately? How did some of you do during the holiday season? I know how one young man did. I can speak of him because I do not know who he was or where he came from, and none of you do. He went home after failing on an examination which he could easily have passed. He had been lazy—that was how the matter stood. Well, a father does not send his boy here to fail on examinations, and when a boy returns home for a holiday after loafing through the term, he ought to be mighty deferential and meek. But the boy plunged into the gayety and danced until two o'clock in the mornings and slept next day until noon, while father was down making bread and butter for the family. Well, Sunday morning came round and that boy was still in bed when the parents returned from church.

"I wonder where George is," his mother asked the father.

"You are asking about the young prince?" the father said. "I think he is yonder in his royal chamber."

There are a lot of young princes like that. Oh, we have all done that sort of thing in all sorts of ways. He does not stand unique. In other words, we have made fools of ourselves. It is very easy for a man to make a fool of himself in this world. It is very easy for him to be caught by the winds of change and whirled about. How is he to save himself from such disaster? "Love doth not behave itself unseemly." Where love is, love will pass the examination, let us say, and not loaf the time away, and love will go home and preserve its self-respect and honor the decencies. Such love never faileth.

Today we are witnessing a great change in religion. Old things are passing away. How are we to keep ourselves steady through the religious upheaval? What are we to tie to when everything, religiously, seems to shift?

Prophecies fail, tongues cease, knowledge passes

away. We have had our fundamentalist prophets and they have failed to satisfy. Their gift of tongues has ceased to work its magic. Their knowledge has vanished away. We are having our modernist prophets and are warming up to their gift of tongues, taking in their knowledge, which will also pass away.

What are we to do among all these prophecies, tongues, knowledges in the name of religion?

Some of my friends are perplexed. Others have given up religion. There is not anything to it, they say.

They are mistaken, according to St. Paul. And he is right. For religion is love. It is a human heart passionately devoted to what is true and good and fair. Such religion, religion as love, never faileth. "We know in part, and we prophesy in part, but when that which is perfect is come, then that which is in part shall be done away."

What is that which is perfect? It is love. And love continues though all else vanishes. The passion for the Godlike endures amidst all the forms and beliefs with which the Godlike is identified. The forms and beliefs are manufactured, and therefore a vanishing commodity. But the Godlike is real.

Religion is love for what is Godlike. You tell me it stands or falls with a theory of Christ's birth? Not at all. You can hold that the Christ came into the world as you did, or that he came here by miracle. It is all one to religion. For religion is love.

You tell me religion stands or falls with a theory of inspiration? Not at all. You can hold that the Bible came down from the skies and that every word is infallible, or you can hold that the Bible has grown, and that its later pages are a finer product than its earlier pages. It is all one to religion. For religion is love, and the Bible is the story of love.

You tell me that religion stands or falls with a theory of the atonement. Not at all. You can hold that Christ's death was a substitution, or that it presents the spectacle of a man serving principle rather than serving policy. It is all one to religion. For religion is love. The great matter in the Christ's death is that there was a man who loved and who loved to the laying down of his life. Get that way of regarding the atonement, and you have something to tie to and be happy in, while the prophets go on with their knowledge and gift of tongues.

That is our great problem today. Can religion survive the world of change? Why of course it can. I mean the religion of love can. That is all there is to religion. "Love never faileth."

And if all the followers of Christ today planted themselves on love, wouldn't everybody be happy and satisfied over religion? There would not be any fighting over it. For love does not fight. But if we make religion a matter of form or method or belief, we will fight the other man who has not our belief or method or form—if he gets in our way.

The other day the *Washington Post* rose up for a great utterance and called for a symposium in answer to the question: "Since everything else has failed, should not religion come to the front and solve the world's problems?"

Well, the symposium was written, and, speaking for myself, it was not enlivening. In the first place, the question was a silly one. If religion is love, what is the sense of asking if love could cure the world's ills?

We all know it could, but we have not reached the stage of love yet. We are at the intellectual stage in religion, and the intellect splits up its world into types that fight each other.

If the *Washington Post* had asked this question: "When are human beings going, or how are they going, to love?" that would have given the preachers something to write about.

We do not love. We love a theory, but that is not love. It is an affection of a certain kind.

One of the writers in that symposium said that the world should get down on its knees and ask God about it. But the world has been on its knees. As I see it, that has been the trouble. The world has been on its knees asking God about it and offering him praise, when what God wants is for the world to get up from its knees and go out and practice the

Godlike. That would be real religion. It would be love, and it would not fail us in our hour of need.

Well, when are we going to get this reign of love that is to handle the great world of change and conflict? I give it up. I do know this—it took the world about a thousand years to exploit religion as an institution. It has been going toward five hundred years since religion has expressed itself as a theory. Looking over history, it would seem as though progress takes a step about every thousand years. At that rate it will be at least five hundred years before we shall reach the end of our sectarian point of view in religion. And even then perhaps the human beings on the earth will not emerge in love.

But the scripture stands. For we know it has it right. Love never faileth. It is the solution of all our world of change. It is the one thing that remains steadfast through the years. The book of Ruth was a sublime love story. It is young and fresh today, after the centuries of change. St. Paul's letters are not remembered much. But this little fragment of writing we call the thirteenth chapter of First Corinthians is remembered and cherished. Why? Because here St. Paul broke forth into light and joy unspeakable. His spirit took wings into the supernal. He was caught up into the indestructible, the immortal world of love.

And as often as we recall his sweet message out

of the Pauline heart, we feel our touch with the wonderful reality of the inner and upper world and are heartened to go on our way in hope.

January 6, 1924

FUNDAMENTALISM AND EVOLUTION: THE BOOK OF JONAH

I SPEAK to you today about a Fundamentalist preacher in the Bible who gave up the ministry because he could not square his Fundamentalism with evolution.

Jonah is his name. The book that records the biography of Jonah is a satirical romance. Through a rare symbolism and sympathetic feeling the author deals with a subject that is as much alive with us today as it was in his day. They were talking about Fundamentalism and evolution ages before Jonah. It was a burning question in Jonah's day. It continues still. Perhaps it will cease some day. Perhaps, I mean, we will all become Christian, yet, and then we will not bother about our Fundamentalism and evolution problem any more.

Our author does not solve the problem. He leaves his hero in distress. The book ends in tragedy—for Jonah.

The Fundamentalist says that we must have something fundamental, permanent, to tie to. The trouble is that he wants us to tie to what he calls fundamental. There is the Baptist Fundamentalist, with his immersion and close communion; the Presbyterian, with his catechism and Thirty-nine Articles; the Catholic, with his Mass. They all have two things in common—one view of creation and one of civilization.

Jonah, then, was a Fundamentalist preacher in Palestine. The Fundamentalist party said that God made the world in six days of twenty-four hours each and then rested from his labors. The final chapter in his task of creation was man. But man went bad. Then God sent a flood and destroyed man, saving one man out of the wreck. This man had three sons. One of them God selected to carry on civilization. He was a Jew. God chose out certain men whom he ordained as priests. They built a church and directed civilization for God. He told them how to proceed and they told the others.

These priests were Jews and salvation was of the Jews. All others were handed over to the uncovenanted mercies. Civilization was to be an enlarged Jewish Empire with God at the head and the sons of Aaron as the administrators of the divine estate. It was a case of Judea over all. The Jews were God's people, therefore, and the others. . . . Well at times they said that the others were their bread. At other times they said that the others were dogs.

But the Modernist party grew up in Judea. They were the prophets. God, according to them, made the world not mechanically but as a process. The world, they said, was an unfolding out of the divine life. And civilization, they said, was a process. It was not of the Jews merely. It centered in the individuals of every race. They substituted self-government for centralized government. And they declared that every little unit of life was as genuinely divine as every other unit. They declared that other units of human life were as genuinely divine as the Judean unit. They were loyal Jews but they were for expansion. "Let us admit the Gentiles," they said. "They are God's people, too."

"How can you admit the Gentiles?" the Fundamentalist asked, "and be a loyal Jew? Is not salvation of the Jews?" In other words, how can you have a civilization that includes both Jew and Gentile? Which will win out? The author of the book of Jonah suggests that neither is obliged to win out, but that the Jew will have to revise his views of God and civilization.

Jonah was a Jewish preacher, and one day he was appointed by his bishop to a church in Nineveh, that old city in Assyria built by Nimrod in the days when man was young.

That was a change for Jonah, and Jonah, being a

Fundamentalist, hated change. He was conservative and wanted to stay in his own state and preach at Capernaum or Sychar or Nazareth. The thought of expansion was abhorrent to him. He did not see how a Jew could acknowledge a Gentile, just as a Presbyterian could not see at one time how he could acknowledge a Baptist.

What did he do? With the spectacle of change before him, he went to the other extreme. Instead of welcoming the change, he went in the other direction. Instead of going east to Nineveh, he went west to Joppa and Tarshish. He would get away as far as he could from the modern movement. When the new style of dress made its first appearance, I knew a woman who was so horrified by it that she made her dress longer and combed her hair back straight. That was a genuine Jonah process. I knew a Fundamentalist preacher in Canada who came South to get away from the Modernists in Canada. The church at one time, seeing the modern tendency, called for more catechism, more family altars, more revivals. Jonah was an unreconstructed Southerner after the Civil War. He was like Senator Lodge and the one hundred per cent Americans after our recent war—get as far away as you can from all forms of modernism. That is going to Tarshish.

But you do not head off change and progress by running away from it. The ancient Fundamentalist writer once said, "Oh that I had wings like a dove!

for then would I fly away, and be at rest." That was a Tarshish experience on the grand scale.

Jonah found a boat in Joppa that was booked for Tarshish in Cilicia, and, buying a ticket, he went on board. But he did not get to Tarshish. He found worse trouble on his hands than he had before he started. And if he had gone to Tarshish he would not have dodged the issue.

On the way something went wrong. One good start wrong deserves another. That is the way of life. Wrongdoing breeds like rabbits. Start out wrong in the morning and the whole day is dogged by the footsteps of that grinning, grunting skeleton.

They struck a storm at sea. There is always that storm at sea when you are going to Cilicia and ought to be in Nineveh.

The sailors, like all seafaring folk, were superstitious and began to worry over the reason for the storm. They knew something was wrong but could not puzzle it out at first. Hitting on the idea that perhaps it was because they had been neglecting their pious devotions, every one of them got down on his knees and began to pray. It must have been a bad storm. I have known people who claimed to be free from what they called the religious experience. But those same people are singularly devout when the electric storm appears over the horizon or a storm of the nature of a fatal physical disease attacks their mortality.

The storm continues on that ship, and, finding that their piety does not still the waves, they turn to science to keep the boat from foundering and throw overboard some of the cargo. It is a case of trusting in God and at the same time keeping their powder dry.

That is good sense. Praying helps, but a bit of practical action helps too. It is good to pray over the broken limb, but it is the sensible thing to call in a doctor. Christian Science has its place, and also the other kind of science.

And still the storm rages. For after all our science, Christian or otherwise, nature has a way of doing as she pleases.

Old sailors say keep on deck in the storm. But Jonah went to his berth as soon as he went on board. (My experience with sea storms is that Jonah was right.) Jonah went to his berth and went to sleep. He was like the men and women around us who are asleep through the stormy and stirring events of their time. He was like some of the students on this campus who are asleep during the great stirring event of these days when the new and greater university is troubling the waters of education in our midst.

The captain at last began to rouse up his passengers and, coming on Jonah, he awakened him and said: "This isn't any time for sleeping. Get up and pray with the others."

Sea captains are masterful people, and Jonah, feeling the imperial hand, gets up and comes on deck.

But instead of being permitted to pray, he is given a questionnaire. Like the little maid who handed the stern questionnaire to St. Peter in the judgment hall, the sailors press Jonah with some significant interrogations. The sailors were superstitious, as we say. For they thought that the storm was due to Jonah; just like Americans who pick up a pin, head first, or who say God worked a miracle to save them in the train wreck when others were killed.

So Jonah tells his story, just like a boy when he comes to the President of the University or the Dean. The interesting thing in Jonah's story is that he says he is from Palestine. He regarded Palestine as God's country and himself as one of God's chosen people. The Palestinians were the Fundamentalists of their day. And yet these pagans, so-called, had more godliness than Jonah. It was a shock to Jonah's Fundamentalism. Here were these pagans—godless people—and there was Jonah, God's man.

> ". . . In even savage bosoms
> There are longings, yearnings, strivings
> For the good they comprehend not."

But they are wonderful in the way they handle the situation. They make Jonah judge in his own case, "What shall we do to thee," they ask, "that the storm may cease?" It was student self-government that prevailed among those pagans on that ship campus.

Jonah is a pretty sick man. A man is a sick man at sea. But Jonah is sick because of memory. His past comes over him now like the past that comes over the man who has fooled in his time and has nothing to show for it when the examination comes. "If I had only played the game instead of playing the fool." That is the way Jonah talks with himself. It is the old story.

Jonah is so sick that he tells the sailors to throw him overboard. Good psychology. He does not mean it, but it makes them want to soften their judgment. And the satire continues. The sailors said: "That's what we ought to do. As a matter of fact you ought to have been thrown overboard when you came on board. But we'll do our best to save you."

Jonah had a chance to learn his good lesson there. He had a chance to learn that the Gentiles—these pagan sailors, for example, and presumably the pagan people of Nineveh—were God's people. He had a chance to learn that civilization is to be judged not in formal terms, but in terms of action. These sailors lacked the form. They were not Jews. But their action was divine. Who are God's people after all? Those who act like God's people. He had a chance to learn that there are other ways to heaven

SERMONS

besides his way. He had a chance to revise his Fundamentalism.

The storm, however, continuing, they finally threw Jonah overboard, and at once the tempest ceased, showing that Jonah was the cause of it!

But our writer is not going to end the story there. The real turn of events, he feels, begins at the point where so many people give up. Brer Fox thought that, when he threw Brer Rabbit in the briar patch, it was all over with Brer Rabbit. But that was the happy moment for Brer Rabbit.

A big fish was swimming around in those waters looking for discarded articles of diet from the ship. This time he found more in the discard than he had contracted for. He found Jonah, and he appropriated Jonah.

Then our hero begins to come to himself. There are two ways in which a man comes to himself. Sometimes he does so through success. Success ruins many a man; but it serves to enlarge and ennoble the lives of others.

Failure is also a form of uplift. Some of us are not any good—and apparently would not be—if we did not get a setback. The prodigal got a six* and immediately came to himself. "How many hired servants of my father's," said the Prodigal, "have bread enough and to spare, and I perish with hunger! I will arise and go to my father."

* "Six" used to be the sign of failure in college courses.

Jonah got a six and came to himself. We read that there within the whale he began to quote Scripture. Hitherto, he had read his Bible as a Fundamentalist, formally. Now for the first time he sees that it has to do with life. A number of Bible passages come to his rescue, and they have real meaning to him now. They bear on his case. One or two of the passages he quotes are significant: "Out of the belly of hell cried I, and thou heardest my voice."

That throws light on the word we call hell. Hell is any wretched condition, such as that in which Jonah found himself.

"They that observe lying vanities forsake their own mercy." That is another quotation. Does Jonah try to see that what he called truth was unconsciously a lying vanity?

The fish finally committed Jonah to the dry land. It is the old story of the reactionary. He finds himself singularly out of place. Palestine got rid of Jonah. Joppa refused to harbor him. The ship refused to carry him. The sea wouldn't have anything to do with him. It committed him to the fish and the fish even regretted its contract.

Our hero is now on land again, and, not waiting to change his clothes, he buys a ticket for Nineveh. For he has another chance to go there. All our fumbling of the ball, you see, all the storms we create and go through—it is all a part of life, and there is progress even in our blunders. Yes, I would say that there is progress even where it looks like total disaster. The moon still remains intact even in total eclipse.

Jonah goes to Nineveh and preaches. But he preaches a message of denunciation. He tells the Ninevites that they are bad, totally bad, and that there isn't any hope for them.

He was like Balaam. Balaam was asked to come and preach against the Jews. But Balaam came and preached in favor of the Jews. Jonah was sent to preach the good news of grace to the Ninevites. But he preached the bad news of total depravity and condemnation. He told the Ninevites that their city was going to be destroyed. Why didn't he go and preach that at first? He tells us. He says he knew that God was so lenient that he would repent and accept the Ninevites. That is why he did not go at first. But after his experience in the deep there wasn't anything left for him but to go. So he went. But he kept the divine mercy quiet. The Fundamentalist dies hard.

God lets lots of people into heaven we would keep out.

Those Ninevites were to be judged in terms of themselves, in terms of their action. Jonah interpreted them in terms of a theory. His theory was that the Jews only were God's people and that all others were bad. But the Ninevites showed by their action that they had good in them and were, therefore, God's people; and so, as his theory fell through, he was discouraged and gave up the ministry. He could not accept the change of view, and God's work went on without him.

A young man went two years ago to study in Yale. He was brought up to look at the Bible and religion in Jonah's way. In Yale they taught him another way. The result is that he is today in Y. M. C. A. work. And he says that he has given up the ministry because he had to give up his religious point of view. A genuine Jonah experience.

Two young men were talking about the Bible and religion the other night. One of them was a Fundamentalist. He believed in the miracle. The other was a Modernist. He said God worked through law and that there could not be any miracle. The former replied that if he believed that he would give up religion. A genuine Jonah experience.

"If my boy can't get an education," a mother said recently, "without going to the University, he will go without an education. For if he goes to the University he will lose his religion and religion is more important than an education." That is a genuine Jonah experience.

The question the story seeks to answer is: How can we allow for change and expansion and still hold on to what we have? You and I have changed and expanded physically since we were babies. We were two or three feet high then. We are from five to six feet high now. Was there anything the matter there? What we had to start with we have. I am I, and you are you, through all the change. The change was not a movement away from what we were. It was a deepening, a growing into what we originally were. The man, the woman, in us emerged into more and more. It did not take wings and fly away.

America has come to the place, lately, where she has gone beyond her Monroe Doctrine. She finds that she has an international life to live. Is she less America than she was? Is she not more? Expanding internationally, she still holds all that America meant, and more than America meant, to Washington and Jefferson and Madison and Monroe.

The Fundamentalist says that God is an infinite Carpenter and that he made the world by miracle and sustains it by miracle. The Scientist says that the world is an evolution. And he knows what he is talking about.

What then? Can we make the change from the Fundamentalist's to the Scientist's point of view and hold to religion? I think we can. But we have to revise our idea of religion; we must have a deeper insight into what is fundamental.

God is not an infinite Carpenter. He is the living God and every little object in the world shares in the divine life. Therefore every movement in nature and human life is a divine movement. That is the

Fundamentalism to tie to, and tying to that, we need have no fear for religion. It brings within the sweep of grace all God's creatures, all objects in space, Ninevites included, as well as Presbyterians and Baptists and Episcopalians and all that comes under the name of our Fundamentalism.

Science? Why Science is one of the great divine movements in the world. Science is simply the attempt to show the orderly arrangement of objects in the world of the living God. The Scientist is not doing away with religion. He is showing how orderly God works; and he is thus deepening and enriching our insight into Reality; he is enlarging the wonder of it all.

So what we need, today, in all this religious controversy, is to enlarge our view of religion. The Fundamentalist has a static view of religion. God is an enlarged Mechanic who made the world by miracle? No. God is the life of the world, and the world is therefore the unfolding of the divine life. No Scientist objects to that. He welcomes it. After all his scientific process, he says that there is that something far more deeply interfused that the religious man calls God and that calls for churches and prayers and hymns and everything that goes by the name of reverence.

The Scientist is right and he knows that he is right. God did not make the world mechanically by miracle. As long as we cling to that, we will have a conflict between science and religion, just like the conflict between Jonah and the modern movement. They will dwell in separate camps, the Fundamentalist discarding science as a bad thing, and the Scientist smiling condescendingly on religion.

Dost thou believe on the Son of man? He answered and said, Who is he, Lord, that I might believe on him? And Jesus said unto him, Thou hast both seen him, and it is he that talketh with thee.—John 9:35-37.

THE EXPRESSION "the Son of man" is sometimes translated the Son of God. The proper reading here is the Son of man. The two expressions are identical.

Dost thou believe on the Son of man? That is the great question of our life. If we are able to answer it, we have entered into our heritage of life.

The question expressed in our own language is something like this: Do you believe in living a man's life? Do you want to be a man?

We are constantly exalting the man Christ Jesus. Why? Because he is the finest exhibition of a man, the de luxe edition of our life. And when Jesus asked his hearers to believe in him, he implied that he wanted them to see their lives mirrored in him. He wanted them not to worship him, but to be men after the manner of man that he proclaimed and illustrated.

Dost thou believe on the Son of man? The question as originally asked grew out of a situation with which we are all familiar. The man thus interrogated had been blind and Jesus had given him his sight. And he had been arraigned before a religious tribunal whose members had bullied him and threatened to cast him out of the church in the hope of getting him to deny that Jesus had healed him. But he stood firm before his accusers, a man, well recommended and of good repute, a man who dared to act as a man even to his own hurt. He was cast out of the church. That was a great disgrace; not only a disgrace, but it meant that he was driven from the presence of God. And this man took his punishment rather than barter his integrity.

Jesus, hearing about what had been done to him and about the splendid manner in which he had behaved, sought him out and had a talk with him. You can imagine the state of mind the man was in. It was the state of mind in which a citizen would be today who had been ostracized by his political friends because he had dared to defend some private interest against the policy of his party. That sometimes happens, and the citizen who comes on that experience undergoes a terrible upheaval. And he needs encouragement in that terrible hour. One of our senators has recently come upon this experience.

Jesus knew what this man was going through and came to him with his encouragement. And the encouragement he brought him was involved in the question: "Dost thou believe on the Son of man?"

It was not so much a question as a positive statement. It was the same as saying: "Yes, they have cast you out of the church, but there is one thing you have left—your integrity. You have taken your life seriously. You have played the man."

The man could have done otherwise. Hailed by that tribunal, he could have answered as his accusers desired and maintained his status in the church. And reading between the lines, it is easy to see that this thought was in his mind. "Dost thou believe on the Son of man?" Jesus asked him. And his reply was, "Who is he, Lord, that I might believe on him?" It was the same as saying, "Yes, I faced the tribunal and did as I did. But I am not so sure that it was worth while. After all, who am I, that I should do as I did? I am only one among so many who think differently. And here I am now a disgraced and ruined man."

But Jesus replied: "It is better to play the man, even if in doing so you have suffered the unhappy consequences. You could have done otherwise and saved yourself. But you wouldn't have saved yourself in the end. No man is satisfied with himself who has acted in that way. What is there to be obtained from standing for one's principles? In a sense, nothing but unhappiness. In a deeper sense, though, is this not what a man's life is? And there is supreme satisfaction in the end in having lived true to the manhood that is in us."

You remember how Jesus once expressed himself on this matter when standing before that same tribunal: "For this cause came I into the world, that I might bear witness to the truth." In bearing witness to the truth, he found his satisfaction, even when he knew that they were getting ready to nail his body to the cross.

You remember what Jesus said on this matter on another occasion: "He that loveth his life shall lose it; and he that hateth his life in this world shall keep it unto life eternal."

And you remember what he said on still another occasion: "Blessed are they which do hunger and thirst after righteousness, for they shall be filled"; and also, "Blessed are they which are persecuted for righteousness' sake, for theirs is the Kingdom of Heaven." He meant that, facing their ordeals as men, they had their citizenship in those divine, heavenly things that are the real marks of a man.

And by way of further encouragement, Jesus declared that he himself was doing what this man had done; yes, and was paying a similar price. He was daring to be a man and was going to keep on daring even if it should cost him his life.

And then it was that the man came to himself and bowed in reverence before the master of men. Yes, and in doing so, he bowed in reverence before the glory of the manhood that was in him. Looking on Jesus and realizing what he stood for, he saw in him a parable of his own life.

The question of Jesus is directed through this man to you and me: "Dost thou believe on the Son of man?" Do we believe in the glory of manhood, our manhood? We have our doubts? Then, do we believe in the glory of manhood as revealed in the person of Jesus? For he is our life in the large. And looking upon the splendor revealed in him, we are obliged to feel the stirring of the splendor within ourselves. Men felt his splendor in the olden time and were moved to dedicate themselves to the things for which he stood. And as long as the memory of him is in the world, men will never be satisfied with themselves as long as they fail to read the parable of their life in him.

I will go further than that. Suppose Jesus had never lived, we are still men. And it is the business of a man to live as a man; just as it is the business of a plant to live as a plant. Long before Jesus lived, men here and there had taken their lives seriously and dared to be men. Daniel for example. Isaiah was another—whose body was finally sawn asunder because he dared to be a man. They had such a man in Athens, who drank the hemlock rather than forfeit his heritage of manhood. Jesus focussed the life of man, hitherto vaguely adjusted. The work of Jesus was to bring men to a consciousness of themselves.

There is a human side to our life, and we are conscious of that. But that is not a man's life. We are human beings with the capacity to serve the right and, therefore, illustrate the divine in our human world.

The man whom Jesus healed was human. He wanted to be like the others around him. He wanted to remain, for instance, in that church and go about from day to day in the favor of his fellow men. But the passion was upon him to do the right. And that passion is the divine in a man. In it we have entered into a holy of holies of life where God has his special dwelling.

The right, you see, is the way we are made. And to live in any other way is to cease to be men. This is the real forfeiture of our lives. We had better be dead men than fail to serve the right. The right is lodged in our lives like the oak in the acorn. It is the task of the acorn to be what it is, an oak. If it fails to be that, it fails utterly. Some acorns become scrub oaks; and that is tragedy for them. Some men become only scrubs; and that is their tragedy.

Jesus is speaking, as usual, this morning on the subject of religion. And religion, as he interprets it, is this passion in man for righteousness. It is therefore not something fantastic, unbelievable, or queer. Neither is it something foreign to our natures or our interests. And to tamper with it is to tamper with the original source and supply of our life. It is our nature to be religious, to serve the divine within us, to serve the right; in other words, to be men. We are on our native heath when we are religious in the sense in which Jesus interpreted religion.

Religion, in his interpretation, is an experience. It is the experience of this man born blind and given his sight. It is the experience of the full-rounded man of whom Jesus speaks when he says that he came to call men to life—the abundant life. To Jesus it was the most wonderful of all experiences, the sublime event in a man's career. Our literary folk speak of the grand passion. The grand passion, to them, is romantic love. But the real romantic love, the real grand passion, is this passion of men for the right, what in our religious dialect we call the passion for God.

We worship God, and that is a beautiful thing. Unfortunately, a lot of religion ends with worship. But real worship is this passion for the right, which is the passion for godliness. It is worship in action, like the devotion a boy has for his mother that shows itself in a daily doing of the things that his mother approves.

This man of whom we are speaking today had not seen that until Jesus showed it to him. He had worshiped God but had never seen that the real worship of God was godliness of life. And the revelation was to him a thrilling experience.

Some years ago a young girl came from a foreign country to study in the University. While in Chapel Hill she visited the various churches but remained a spectator of religion. Being asked on one occasion about her view of religion, she said her father had asked her to study the churches with a view to finding out which she thought had the correct religion. Her father, she said, was a busy man who had not had time to be religious, and, as he anticipated retiring from business, he hoped to pay attention to religion in the future spare time he was to have on his hands.

She expressed a great admiration for the way her father lived. She said he always tried to do the fair thing in his transactions with his fellow men, that he was most devoted to the interests of his home, and was always ready to serve those who called on him for help. And when she was told that that was what Jesus meant by being religious, she lapsed into silence for a moment, and then replied: "I have always believed something like that, and when I go back home I'm going to tell my father that he has always been a religious man."

That situation and the conversation that grew out of it were similar to the situation and conversation on the ancient ground of Palestine when Jesus talked with the man who had been cured of his blindness.

This man had been brought up in the Jewish faith. In the olden days the Jew had been taught that God had his special dwelling in a place called the holy of holies in the east end of the temple.

It was a wonderful distinction these ancient people drew between the holy place in the temple and the holy of holies there, even if it was a formal way they had of stating the relation between God and man.

The holy place was the outer court into which the people came for worship. The holy of holies was the inner court where God dwelt, and into which only the high priest could enter, and that only once a year. The holy place was for men. The holy of holies was for God. The one was a human place. The other was divine. Thus the two places were separated, God remaining in his own region and men in theirs. In those ancient times they separated God and man, the divine and human.

But one day the temple was destroyed with its holy of holies. Those unhappy people were carried into captivity. In captivity they conceived a new way of interpreting the relation between God and man. Returning from captivity, they brought with them a body of law. And then they identified God with the law. The law became the holy of holies where God dwelt. And the scribe or lawyer became the high priest, standing between the holy of holies of the law and the human being.

Such was the faith of the Jew in the days of the

New Testament. And this young man cured of his blindness had been brought up on that faith. There was the holy of holies called the law, and there was this man who had defied the law. Yes, and there he was with the condemnation of the law upon him, cast out of the church, a renegade, like a man cast out of his political party today.

But Jesus, as it is beautifully said by one of his biographers, broke down the middle wall of partition between God and man, between the divine and the human. He claimed to be a man, but he also claimed that a man's life was inherently divine. Going about among his fellow beings, he was human in every way, touched with a feeling of men's infirmities. But wherever he went, his human relations were touched and hallowed by the life of the divine from within. This is what St. John meant when he wrote: "In him was life, and the life was the light of men." "We beheld his glory, the glory as of the only begotten of the Father, full of grace and truth."

At last this great high priest has appeared, touched with the feeling of human infirmities, who has opened the door leading into the holy of holies of the temple of a man's life. And in the joy of the holy of holies experience this man bows in reverence before the high priest of his heart. The poor fellow, like the young girl mentioned, had had inklings hitherto in his soul of something like that and needed only the word of Jesus to bring it into perspective.

A great many books have been written on the divinity of Jesus. But one book remains to be written, which, when written, will show that human nature is inherently divine. And, like that man given his sight, every time a human being lives true to the best within him, he is displaying divinity after the manner of the divine man, Christ Jesus.

We can be human and barter our convictions for the sake of our safety. But the divine in a man, when released, will never permit him to barter his convictions, no matter what the safety. The senator in Congress who has lately expressed his convictions against the majority of his party on matters that concern the public welfare may not see clearly into the matter at issue. But he sees that Congress must serve the people or become a joke. And in seeing that and speaking his mind upon it, he has brought God within the holy of holies of his life and illustrated him within the precincts of our congressional temple.

We can be human and declare when we have a moral collapse, like the people in the Garden of Eden, that it was due to our environment. But the divine in a man, when released, will never permit him to say that he is a product of his environment. A man is a man, despite all that his environment does to him. And when the youth who once failed to make good on this campus told his parents that it was his own fault and wanted another chance, he placed himself in the line of apostolic succession with the man cured of his blindness, and with the person of Jesus who effected the cure. He could have said that he could not study or keep his character in the atmosphere of the University. But it takes a man to say what he did.

We can be human and fuss over the unhappy conditions of our life, striking back at those who have struck at us, complaining of our hard lot, becoming embittered by our sorrows. But the divine in us, when released, will lay its hand deftly, courageously, and unerringly upon the worst condition of our life, translating it from being a master into a servant. So that if our enemy hunger, we will feed him; and if he thirst, we will give him drink; so that in the face of suffering, we will see the joy that has been set before us; and in our griefs, we will find our strength.

Much has been said and written of late about relativity, and the moral code, like other things in the world, has been spoken of as a relative thing. The idea of such teaching is that a man should tell the truth or do the right thing toward his fellow man except when haled before a tribunal—as in the case of the man born blind. The idea is, do the right thing except when you see trouble ahead. Then compromise, or in some way do the other thing so that you may save yourself. The idea is, when in pain cry out, become petulant, instead of being schooled through pain.

To the pure soul of Jesus, such doctrine was not only a travesty on human intelligence, but an abominable way for a man to treat his life. And to men everywhere, especially to those who find themselves in the fierce struggle of life and who have, perhaps, here and there let down the ideal to follow the primrose path of dalliance, the question of Jesus comes ringing over the centuries: "Dost thou believe on the Son of man?"

IMMORTALITY

Jesus Christ . . . who hath brought life and immortality to light.—2 Timothy 1:10.

THIS IS our Easter message—immortality. It is a message we do not preach on often enough. But it is one on which we shall preach with greater emphasis as we come to realize what Christianity is. The Gospel message is that a man's life has value and permanency in itself. It is not a product.

The question of immortality is bound up with this larger question: namely, has a human being any value in himself, or is he simply a product? In other words, is a human being real, fundamental, or is he here by courtesy? If a man is a product of his environment, the question of his continuance after death is settled forever in the negative. There is nothing fundamental in him and therefore nothing permanent about him. And that is a view that is as old as man himself and that has been stated in various ways and at various times all down through the past. It has been stated with such emphasis these latter days that it is doubtless the reason why so many men have come to take it for granted that this life is possibly all there is. It is doubtless the reason for the religious indifference that attaches itself to our age as contrasted with the preceding age.

The ancient Hindoo had the thought of man as a product. A man counted for nothing in himself. To the Hindoo there was but one reality—God. And a man was not only not real, but his life was a tragic thing until he lost himself in the life of God. The hope and ambition of the Hindoo was Nirvana. The curse of life to the Hindoo, as it is the joy of life to the Christian, was to be an individual.

The ancient Hebrew had the suggestion of the individual. To the Hebrew mind God only was real, but a man could share in the life of Jehovah. He could achieve citizenship in the Kingdom of God. And in proportion as he did so his life became real. The Hebrew, however, had but a faint suggestion of immortality. He had no thought of immortality in the sense in which the Christian has come to employ the term. His was the thought—crudely and vaguely expressed—of physical immortality. The author of the Book of Job, who possibly wrote near the New Testament times, asks the question: "If a man die, shall he live again?" And his answer? "There is hope of a tree, if it be cut down, that it will sprout again . . . but man dieth and wasteth away . . . and where is he?"

According to the Hebrew a man was the product of his environment. His environment was God. God made him and it was with God to do with him of his own pleasure. God was represented on earth by the church. If a man joined the church and did the works ordained by God, he became a sharer in what God chose to give him. When the divine government was some time to be established on earth, the Jew was to have his place there along with all who had been baptized in the Jews' faith. There is the suggestion in all this that a man's life was real and a suggestion of immortality.

The Greek had a similar suggestion. God to him was the supreme idea of the world. Very early in his thinking, he drew the distinction between the ideal world and the world of man, and he said that man received value only as he shared in the ideal. The way to share in the ideal was through mathematics, and only the mathematicians went to heaven. The man himself was not real. It was only the ideal element in him that was real and that gave him whatever value he had. "A man is known by the company he keeps"—that was the philosophy of the Greek. There is an ideal world of which men may partake, and men are known only because of that good company they may keep. The ideal continued but the man died. "Some little talk awhile of ME and THEE there was—and then no more of THEE and ME." The Greek thought ended in Stoicism and the Stoic was hopeless of the future. Rare men among them wrote beautifully of a life after death, but as Zeller, the great modern interpreter of the Stoic, points out, it was not the conception of immortality that we enjoy as Christians.

Our modern materialistic scientist—and science is not all materialistic—teaches that a man is a by-product. It is the modern equivalent of ancient Greek thought. It is quite a common saying today that a man is what he is because of the forces that have played and are playing about him. A man is an empty vessel. In himself and of himself he can do no good thing. All we can say of the world, including our own part in it, is that everywhere an infinite and eternal energy prevails. That alone is real. Men may come and men may go but it alone goes on forever. All else is but the manifestation of that ceaseless, tireless energy. Our lives are but as the waves of the ocean, the ripples on the stream. We are but parts of nature, as the arms and limbs are parts of the body. Our brain secretes thought and emotion and moral action as the digestive system secretes its juices. All our fine feelings, our affections, our achievements, our moral splendor, our systems of thought, our art, our religion—it is all a secretion, a product. It depends altogether on the impulses that come in on us from without, through our senses, and that disturb the tissue of the brain. There is no hope anywhere.

> "We are no other than a moving row
> Of Magic Shadow-shapes that come and go
> Round with this Sun-illumined Lantern held
> In Midnight by the Master of the Show."

It is very interesting to reflect that the Christian Church has also taught this doctrine, that a man is a product, that he has nothing in himself of permanent value. The universe is but a fleeting show. Life is a vain, empty thing. The world is very evil. Only God is real, and he has made man, and a man may find his way into the world of God if he just stops thinking that he is real and takes on the plan of salvation that has been handed down to him out of heaven. When you die—even though you do not deserve it—you will find your heaven because you have exercised faith.

The great Cardinal Newman accepted the teaching of modern materialistic science that a man is nothing in himself, that he is just a product. What then? Skepticism? No. Cast yourself on the church and its deposit of doctrine received from the Apostles and Fathers who received it from God. Don't ask any questions about it. Only have faith.

But everywhere the thoughtful man is restless today, unsatisfied, vaguely groping about looking for a message that will help him to solve the great problem of change and give him comfort in the presence of the great change that overtakes every man at last. As much as the Christian Church has tried to meet the situation, she has failed. And she has failed because she has never yet looked the problem squarely in the face. If a man is a product, the matter ends there. There is literally no hope for him. In the words of the old Persian, he comes like water, and he goes like the wind. You and I either have something real within us or we have not. If we have not, we are here only by courtesy. We are not necessary to life, and God could not give us immortality if he would. It is not conferred. And we need not look expectantly forward. But if we have that real nature within us, even the gates of death cannot prevail against us.

History is the perpetual witness to the inherent value and dignity of human life. History has issued in the Christian movement; and as much as the Church has misunderstood it and still misunderstands it—and the scientific student has ignored it—the doctrine of Christianity is that a human being is a center of life, a center of reality; that he has something within him that is his very own, not something isolated, apart, but something that shares in the life of reality. "Jesus Christ, who hath brought life and immortality to light." Jesus Christ, in other words, found men to be real, and once you grant that a man is real, you acknowledge his permanence; you acknowledge that there is that in him that survives all change, even the last great change itself. It is wonderfully said that Jesus Christ brought this life to light, who hath brought reality and immortality to life. Reality was already there—latently, implicitly there. He only found it there and coaxed it out into the open. He only awakened men to a consciousness of it. He did not confer it upon men. He developed it within them as the gardener develops the blossom from the rose, as the teacher develops the thought within the mind of the student. In another place it is said, "I am come that they might have life." He came to stimulate, to arouse, to make active the reality within men; and once that active life principle is made active within us, we become the witnesses of our permanence. They said of Jesus Christ that it was not possible that he should be holden of death. Why? Because he himself was a center of life, a center of reality. He lived his life as such, and lived it so perfectly that they recognized in him that which defied all change.

The teaching of Jesus was that a man is a child of God. As such he partakes of the nature of God. He is divine, and the divine is permanent. And man as God's child is permanent. He is in the world to stay. The ravages of time cannot destroy him. Death becomes an open door, not an impassable wall. We have only to examine our lives to find permanence there. Take our power to know. Men as thinking beings have found themselves sharers in the infinite, the eternal world of truth. Truth is not something conferred on a man, to be taken away at will. It is a man's life. "I am the truth," said Jesus Christ. Man is truth, and as truth he enjoys immortality.

Take our power to do the right. A man has capacity for character. It is not something conferred on him which can be taken from him as a parent takes candy from a child. It is his life. He is born to live as such. Jesus Christ brought this capacity of a man to the light, and there it has shone ever since; and man as a character enjoys immortality. That is something that cannot have a funeral.

Take our power to feel. A man can love. He is built along the lines of pure, disinterested feeling, and can love to the laying down of his life. No one has conferred that capacity on him. He has it as a child of God, and in his enjoyment of it he has immortality. The great Jonathan Edwards, in a message to his wife shortly before his death, made this marvelous Christian statement: "The uncommon union which has so long existed between us has been of such a nature as I trust is spiritual and therefore will continue forever." One can forgive Jonathan Edwards for much of his harsh teaching. That also is Christ's statement about a man. He has brought life and therefore immortality to light. He has discovered that men are centers of life, that they

SERMONS

have within them, as flames struck out from the central fire, all the nature of that central fire; or, to change the figure, moving about amidst things seen and temporal, they have vital intercourse with that which is not of time or place, that which reaches out into the infinite and eternal.

A poet once wrote: "On earth our erring fingers touch the chords that send a thrill throughout infinity." Yes. It is even so. On earth, living in these physical tabernacles, we are also sharers by our very nature in that which endures. Living in a world of change, we carry with us all the way along that which knows no change, that which survives all change, that which is above all change. And just as we go to our sleep and rise again conscious of who we are, and never mistake ourselves for others, so may we confidently say that when we lie down at last in the sleep of death, we shall still have our permanence, even as our dust returns to its kindred dust.

It is just as silly to deny immortality as it is to deny the chimpanzee. The chimpanzee has arrived. There he is. At any rate this is the direction that history has taken and the spirit of history is always right. The Christian movement has come into the world, a necessary part of the world process, not only so, but apparently the final chapter in that process; and it is our privilege today to stand up in the courage and joy of the Christian message:

"Jesus Christ, who hath brought life and immortality to light."

The question of immortality today becomes for you and me this question: not, shall I continue after death; not, shall I know my comrades in another world—but, shall I live now and here as a man may live, as a man is born to live? We are born immortal. But I have seen men born with business capacity who threw their heritage to the winds and died in poverty. I have seen men born to be leaders who squandered their birthright and died not even good followers. I have seen men born to high places in the world who took very low places, and while we are all of us centers of reality—candidates for immortality—we may live as the animals, simply organisms. And whatsoever a man soweth, that shall he also reap.

Let us take the Easter message home with us today and see to it that the stamp of it is henceforth upon our life. Let us labor to do the task that lies to hand as the task should be done—perfectly; let us strive in all our conduct to do the right. Let truth be our aim, though all our prejudices and theories must be flung to the winds. Above all, let love and joy and peace and sweetness and tenderness and service and all holy affections become the daily comrades of our life. Thus may the Christ be formed within us; thus may he bring within us life and immortality to light.

And I John saw the holy city, new Jerusalem, coming down from God out of heaven, prepared as a bride adorned for her husband. . . . The length and the breadth and the height of it are equal.—Revelation 21:2, 16.

THE AUTHOR of the book of the Revelations wrote as a Christian in a pagan world. The pagan was a villager, whose horizon was bounded by his own local interests. The Roman in whose world our author lived was a villager on a large scale. Civilization, to him, was identified with the Roman state.

A Christian is first a man and afterwards a villager. He believes in men and in a civilization that has its source in men and that exists for men, not for any class of men. He has the local interest like that of the pagan, but he brings to the local interest the vision and fervor of the cosmic mind. As we would say in the language of the street, he is a great big kind of a man. In other words, he has risen above the dead level of material existence into the full, free, joyous experience of life. He is purged from his obsessions. He has passed beyond the meager into the abundant manner of living.

Our author is telling us what society will be like when it becomes Christian. "I John saw the holy city, new Jerusalem, coming down from God out of heaven, prepared as a bride adorned for her husband"; and "The length and the breadth and the height of it are equal."

We speak, continually, of Christian civilization. According to Jesus, civilization is Christian by nature, and all we need to do to it is to shape it into what by nature it was intended to be.

When a man becomes a Christian, he becomes what his constitution as a man calls for, just as in growing into a physical being he carries out the plan of his cellular structure. And in attempting to inject the Christian principle into human affairs, our aim is to effect a constitutional state of society. The men who, in the Philadelphia Convention, conceived our constitution saw what Jesus saw when, having called his apostles together, he preached to them his Sermon on the Mount. Christianity, therefore, is not a dream of Utopia. It is a vision of society to which we, as American citizens, are committed.

Our author writes of civilization as a city, and he tells us that when the city of civilization is raised, the length and the breadth and the height of it will be equal.

The length—there we have the expansion of men's individual interests. It contains the idea of self-development, men reaching out from themselves to become more of themselves, the right of the human being to life, liberty, and the pursuit of happiness.

The breadth of the city—there we have the spectacle of men concerned for the common weal. And this means that the human being, seeking his own, toiling to place himself in the sun, also hears the still, sad music of humanity, and is jealous to conserve the welfare of others, is sensitive to his responsibilities as well as his rights.

The height of the city—there we have the expansion of men's ultimate and inner life. And this means that in the city of civilization the human being, seeking his own and finding himself in a community of lives, has the sense of justice that enables him to preserve the relation between private and public good.

History, which is the story of the city of civilization, is a highway cluttered with wrecks of the builder's art. For the symmetry of length and breadth and height has never been wrought out. The length has been there without the breadth or the height, or the breadth without the length and height. And the height has never yet risen into any appreciable prominence.

Christianity stressed the height along with the

breadth and the length. It injected the sense of justice into human affairs. And its golden teaching is that if justice be in the hearts of a people, from that lofty elevation of experience they have such a clear vision of the landscape of their life that they are going to write justice into their private and public deeds.

History ran its gamut in the career of the Hebrew people. All the elements of civilization are there for our beholding. And as these ancient folk had a career similar to our own, we cannot do better, this morning, than review their story as they struggled to place civilization on the earth.

Our first contact with them is in their ancestral home of Babylonia, where they were ruled with an iron hand, similar to the iron rule that prevailed in Europe before our ancestors left its shores. At last, finding the conditions of their life intolerable in that old world, we find the Hebrews trekking in covered wagons to the land of Canaan, which was the America of that ancient time.

They were thus the original Pilgrim Fathers, who, before even pitching their tents on the land of their adoption, bowed their heads in a prayer of consecration. And there, as they prayed, they vowed to build a city of civilization whose length and breadth and height should be equal, a city in which the spirit of justice should flourish as the green bay tree and where, therefore, the individual should be free and accord freedom to his fellow man. Such was the nature of the Abrahamic covenant chronicled later in the sacred annals, the second of which became the written constitution of the Hebrew people. It contained the vision of a commonwealth.

Abraham was the leading Pilgrim Father of his day, who beheld the city of civilization not yet translated into bricks and mortar and pavements. And under the spell of his vision the Hebrews laid out the length of their city, enjoying for the first time in their history a career of freedom, no one daring to molest them or make them afraid.

Then came Moses and others after him, through whom the building material of thirteen colonies was finally collected, if we include the two half tribes of Joseph. These all had vision of the breadth as well as the length of the city. They saw that to live in freedom men must live in unity.

Now they had length and breadth, and yet they were at war. The height had to come in to complete the task. This was achieved by David. But David never concluded the job of the height of the city. Mounting the throne, he ruled as a Babylonian monarch, making the people his subjects. He brought about a condition like that expressed by Louis XIV when he said: "I am the state." He was the King George III over those thirteen colonies. His office became hereditary like that of the British sovereign, and his successor became so fired with the obsession of power that the people under his rule were as though they were not. Ahab finally became so drunk with the sense of power that he brought on a revolution similar to that of the Boston Tea Party and the Revolutionary War, to which that party was a prelude.

Three lessons, however, the Hebrew people learned, although they had not succeeded in working them out. They learned that the city of civilization must have length and breadth and height. And, having come on a state of bankruptcy, they were ready to start the task over again. And their fresh beginning took the form of a revolutionary war.

That war was led by the prophet and in that war the Hebrews asserted their ancient right to life, liberty, and the pursuit of happiness, guaranteed by the constitution left them by their father Abraham. The prophet was the Patrick Henry of those days, who preferred death with liberty to life without it. And from Ahab forward, the idea of liberty continued to be the prominent theme of the people.

The revolution begun in the days of Ahab was not completed for a long period. But they finally fought their revolutionary war with success, and after it was over they assembled to confer upon the next step the builders should take in the construction of the city of civilization.

This assembly was of the nature of our Philadelphia Convention, and the net result of its proceedings was that they reaffirmed their belief in constitutional government. The sovereignty with its imperialism was at an end. They were going to live together as a community of individuals, not as subjects of a king.

They needed a man to guide them in that crucial hour, and they found him in the person of Nehemiah, who became the George Washington of the young state. But when Nehemiah set to work to bring constitutional government to pass, he had as difficult a task on his hands as the Father of our country. A community is composed of individuals who, like the atoms in space, have a way of dividing into groups. And after a time this very thing happened on the soil of Judea.

Instead of constitutional government they had a government based on class distinction. A group of men rose into power and seized the reins of government. And they became the legislators of the young state. It was a parliamentary, not a constitutional, government. It centered in the hands of a legislature on which there were no checks, and its members appointed their successors in office. The people were called together by Nehemiah and asked to vote for what they wanted. But the party that had risen into power had entrenched itself so strongly that the power in its hands had become hereditary. A system of nepotism prevailed; and the people were under the iron rule of a legislative group whose interest lay in keeping themselves in power, not in serving the needs of the people.

There were men within that legislative body who had a broader outlook and who had a generous thought about the needs of the people. But gradually great estates emerged that threw in their influence with the majority in power. One of these great estates was owned by the sons of Annas. Annas was the speaker of that ancient assembly whose deliberations were controlled by him and his sons. And the names of Annas and his sons became heralded abroad as synonymous with all that was ignoble and brutal and mean.

The press of the day was employed in the service of the ruling class. A group of writers emerged who backed up the policy of the administration by annotating and codifying the laws that had been enacted for the people, showing that those laws were ordered of God and made in heaven. And a group of historical writers appeared who sought to show the people that the rule of Annas and his sons was in line with the ancient policy of those who had fought the revolutionary war. The result was that the dream of constitutional government was on the rocks.

Two steps, however, had been taken in the city of civilization. The people had learned that there was such a thing as individual liberty. They learned that lesson in their revolutionary war against the sovereign. In other words, they had learned that the city must have length.

But in working out their liberty they had learned that they had moral obligations to sustain. They learned that lesson through Isaiah and also through Nehemiah, who called them together in convention. And even though their moral obligations had been misinterpreted as loyalty to a class, they had learned that there was such a thing as a community and such a thing, therefore, as moral behavior. They had learned that the city must have breadth.

And hence the struggle that had set in between the interests of the individual on the one hand, and the interests of the community on the other; between individual rights and moral responsibility; between the length and the breadth of the city of civilization. A general murmur of discontent prevailed on every hand. Skepticism of government here and there broke out in rabid form. Even revolution was attempted. And all the time the ruling class, representing the community, went on as though nothing were happening. There was a daily newspaper in Jerusalem in those days. It would be enlivening to know what it had to say. But at any rate the press, in the form of philosophical and historical textbooks, continued to flood the country with statements of how splendidly government was being carried on, how everything was going as it should, how good times were in sight, as was the peace, perfect peace, that flows like a river.

Jesus was born in the city of civilization when this conflict between the individual and the community was at its height. As he grew up in the little obscure town of Galilee, he heard much talk by his elders about the sad manner in which public affairs were being managed in Palestine. And, coming to man's estate, he became aware of the rift between the people and their rulers, not merely between the Jewish people and the Roman state, but between the Jewish people and the Jewish state that existed within the Roman territory. But his concern was with his own state and his own people. When he was only a lad his parents took him on one occasion to the capital, and while there he asked of those who were guiding the affairs of state some pointed questions that failed to secure a satisfactory answer. He was then only twelve years of age, but a precocious youth of that age can ask unanswerable questions of his seniors.

Returning home, he worked in his father's carpenter shop until he was thirty years old. We have no record of what went on in his mind during that interval. But it is evident that he was thinking and coming to definite conclusions, for at thirty years of age he was taking a vital interest in public affairs. And it was not long before the young men of the time flocked to his side.

While attending a great mass meeting in the capital, a young man called on him at the home where he was being entertained, and the enthusiasm over him of the younger generation was expressed by that youth, who wanted him to launch a revolution: "No man can do these miracles you are doing except God be with him. Why, then, do you not become our leader and break the power of our oppressors and set us free?"

This young man, like those radiant spirits that emerge among us from time to time, was for inaugurating a new party in the state. Every little while a new party is launched on our soil. The latest attempt along this line was made by a distinguished professor of one of our universities. But we have about come to the place where we have ceased to hope in the efficacy of a party to save us.

Jesus had already arrived at that place. And in his memorable conversation with that youth he states his conviction on this matter: "Except a man be born again, he cannot see the Kingdom of God." The idea was that the country was sufficiently organized. There were the two great parties in the strife, the people on the one hand seeking their rights, and their representatives on the other administering those rights in the interests of their own idea of government.

And Jesus declared that what was needed in that deadlock was not heat but light, not war but co-operation, not force but truth. His attitude was similar to that of Isaiah under similar circumstances: "Come now, and let us reason together, saith the Lord; though your sins be as scarlet, they shall be as white as snow; though they be red like crimson, they shall be as wool." In other words, he was for returning to first principles, for harking back to the idea of constitutional government announced by the ancient Pilgrims who trekked from Babylonia to Canaan.

Those Jewish people had carried a false view of life with them since the days their ancestors landed at their Plymouth Rock in Canaan. It was the view that when two forces are pitted against each other, one of them is obliged to yield to the other. Finding their individual liberty, they thought that the next step was to fight their social obligations. And now, having effected a social status, those who administered it were for fighting the individual who was not satisfied with it.

In other words, in laying out the length of the city of civilization, they denied a place to the breadth. And now, having laid out the breadth, those who did so were denying a place to the height.

But Jesus called their attention to the height. Length without breadth, he declared, was futile. And breadth without length was futile. Both were necessary to a finished city. And it is only as the height raises its head on the horizon that both can be sustained. He held the view that where two forces are in conflict with each other, both are valid and should be encouraged to co-operate with each other. And this called for the spirit of justice in those who were at war.

And justice, as Jesus taught it, is not a mere sentiment. It is sentiment growing out of thought and truth. It is a case of "Come, now, let us reason together."

There are two views of human nature. According to one view, it is black; according to the other, it is white. Jesus taught that it was white with black spots on it. Annas and his sons who were administering the affairs of the Jewish state had black spots on them, let us say, large black spots. But Jesus declared that the white was there underneath the black.

It is the fashion always for men to turn on those in power. Civilization has thus always been a matter of ins and outs. But those who are out of power are exactly like those who are in power. Place power in the hands of any man, and in ninety-nine cases out of a hundred he is going to misconceive its nature and misuse it.

When men rise into power, you see, they have a most difficult task on their hands. And it is no wonder that they misconceive its nature and put it to a wrong use. They do so, not because they are bad, but because they are not sufficiently grown into the sense of justice to know what to do in their situation. And as something must be done, they do the thing that they think will secure the best results. Unfortunately, those results are always unfair to somebody involved in the transaction.

The paramount element in public affairs that has, therefore, been given but a fitful chance is the element of justice. But it is the one element that if given a chance is triumphantly satisfactory. For it is the truth put to work. The truth put to work is the right, and the right is God, and even one with God is a majority.

The decisions of John Marshall stand, for they are constitutional and therefore right. They were satisfactory to all concerned, and they are satisfactory still. Looking back on them, we are proud of that chapter in our history. Our advent into the Philippine territory was of this nature. We had no other desire than to serve the cause of the Filipinos in particular and of humanity in general. And it is proving satisfactory.

We have done a number of things as a nation with which we do not feel satisfied, and it is because they were not done right.

Individually, men of any degree of self-respect spurn to do anything but what is just. There is a beautiful give and take among us in our various communities. Ambitious, we conserve the rights of others. And rising into financial or social power, we are wonderfully generous toward our less fortunate neighbor.

There is no reason why we should not bring justice to pass in our public as well as in our private life. And all we need to bring it to pass is simply to remember that we are still men dealing with men while dealing with them in a public manner.

A business man sometimes cheats in business. All he needs, however, is to remember that he is first a man, doing business with the sense of justice in his life. With that memory upon him, he will be as white in business as he is in his daily social intercourse.

A man in political life sometimes uses his opportunity to further his own interests or the interests of his party. But all he needs to remember is that he is first a man and afterwards a political power. With the sense of manhood within him, which is the spirit of justice, he will serve his state in as manly a manner as he is ready to serve his next door neighbor.

There are many interests among us. The farmer has one. His tenant has another. There is the interest of the policeman, who is the pastor of our pavements, and the interest of the community that hires and pays the policeman. There is the interest of the man who runs the place of industry, and the men who help him to run it. The lawyer has his interest, and the client has his. The country is full of teachers and doctors and business men and preachers and schools and churches and canals and railroads and automobiles and airplanes, of little, obscure folk and folk in the limelight, of smart people and dull people, yes, the bad as well as the good. There are states and commonwealths of states. There are consumers and manufacturers.

The world is full of interests. The world we call ours is full of interests. And the teaching of Jesus is that all interests count. The little part's interest counts, and the interest of the whole of society of which it is a part also counts. And the spectacle of one interest pitting itself against the whole, or of the whole working against the one, is a spectacle of the jungle, whose citizens tear each other in the slime, not of civilization, which is composed of men made in the image of God and capable of big, high passions.

And I believe we are entering upon a new era in history, when the philosophy of the jungle is to be replaced by a nobler philosophy. The philosophy of the jungle is that when two interests clash, one must yield. The nobler philosophy is that when two interests clash, they do so because they have failed to understand each other. And where war has been the order of the civilization of the past, co-operation is to be the order of the future. And in this we are but recording afresh the vision of the ancient seer of Patmos: "I John saw the holy city, new Jerusalem, coming down from God out of heaven, prepared as a bride adorned for her husband"; and "The length and the breadth and the height of it are equal."

I will lift up mine eyes unto the hills, from whence cometh my help.—Psalm 121:1.

THIS IS the glory of the Bible. The men who wrote its pages wrote out of a great experience. This is why it has gone down in history as our sacred book. "Sacred" means fundamental. The Bible is a fundamental book.

The man who wrote the 121st Psalm had a fundamental experience. Like others about him, he was a citizen of the world and engaged in the enterprise of daily living, making a livelihood, attending to duties of various kinds, sustaining the relations that crowd in upon the human being from every source. But in and through these minor experiences he had a great experience that he expressed when he said: "I will lift up mine eyes unto the hills, from whence cometh my help."

Our life is a landscape of hills and plains, and our daily and minor experiences represent the plain country, while the great experience represents the

I will lift up mine Eyes—
hills etc. PS 121

1. Theory
2. Form
3. Exper.
   Sense of law

This is the glory of the Bible. The men
who wrote its pages wrote out of a [real?]
presence. This is why it has come
down in history as our Sacred book.
"Sacred" means fundamental. The B. is
a ^truly book.

The man who wrote the
121st psalm had a fundamental
experience. Like others about him
he was a citizen of the [world?] & engaged in the enterprise of daily
living, making a livelihood, attending
to duties of various kinds, sustaining
the relations that crowd in upon
the he being from every side
But in & thro these [minor?]
experiences he had a great
experience that he expressed
when he said: "I will lift [up?]"
our life is a landscape of hills & plains
and these daily common or en-
periences represent the plain
country while the sky & sky, & [lofty?] hills
in the landscape.

hills. Once a man sees that and acts upon it, he sees the whole story of his life.

What a dreary monotonous thing our world would be if it were all plain territory. I was brought up on the western plains,* but I always missed something in that landscape and knew not what I missed until I found myself one day where the hills lifted their heads above the plains.

The people who dwell amidst the hills have also something left out of their landscape and grow isolated in consequence. And the man whose inner landscape is only one of hills lives an isolated life. He has visions and dreams but fails to translate his visions and dreams into action. But our interest is in the other man this morning, the man who has not found his citizenship in the hills.

In nature the plains and hills commingle so that you cannot tell where the hill leaves off and the plain country begins, or the plain leaves off and the ascent begins.

Everything in nature is the servant of a higher power. The drop of water is not only wet but has within it the higher qualities of oxygen and hydrogen. The grain of wheat contains the high potentiality of vegetation. And the human being comes into the world endowed with a transcendent power. There is the plain surface of a human experience

---

* Some of us remember that Moss said, "At the age of three I moved to the western plains, taking my parents with me."

and also the altitudes, the plateaus and also the prairies, the lower and also the higher level. We can live on the surface of life. A great many people do. They live between their homes and their places of business, with no light in their eyes as they go to and fro upon their patch of earth. They teach, or toil at their desks or on the streets, as servants of the place that commands their interest, seeing no farther than their eyes behold. This is what has been called the superficial life—the life that runs with the regularity of the plain country. But we also speak of the serious life. And the serious life is one that sees the high in the lowly, the grandeur in the commonplace, the possibility in the unfinished, the hope where despair lifts up its head—the man, namely, who brings to his daily contacts the sense of elevation.

The sense of elevation in a man's life is what we know as a religious experience. It is the presence of God in a human heart. Did we have a sense of elevation at any time in our experience this past week? Let us put that down as once, at least, when we had a religious experience, when we looked on the face of God.

Men ask all manner of questions about religion, about God, about Christ, about the Bible, about the church and its ceremonies, about miracles, about immortality. But religion is an experience. It sits enthroned in the heart of a man every time he looks up from any commonplace relation to behold the higher and wider horizon in which that relation is set. Religion, therefore, does not depend on anything outside of us, while using every outside aid. If there were not any Bible or any church or any preachers or any theology, men would still be religious. For they have within them this wondrous capacity to see bigger than their eyes behold. At one time there was not any Bible or church or preacher or theology. There were just men. And, having in their hearts the power to see in the high and large, as well as in the low and meager manner, they sought the high and large—they became religious. And out of that religious experience grew the Bible and the church and the preacher and the theology.

Having this capacity for high things, a man is by nature religious. He is first a son of God and second a religious man, answering the call of that which is higher than himself, as the plant answers the call of the principle of vegetation within it, or the animal answers the call of the instincts with which it is endowed.

The Psalmist is telling us how natural a thing religion is in a man's life. "I look up to the hills," he declares, "from whence cometh my help." And then he goes on to say: "My help cometh from the Lord, which made heaven and earth." In other words, the hills stand to the plains as the high things of life—the things of God—to our daily and minor experiences.

Any sense of elevation a man enjoys is God in that man's life. It is a religious experience, so that religion becomes, to the man who has it as an experience, a daily habit. And men often illustrate religion even when denying its reality. What they deny is not religion but some form of religion. I had a great friend some years ago who has passed into the great unknown. He used to tell me that he did not see anything in religion. But he was one of the most religious men I have ever known. For he practiced religion. He had it as an experience. He was a business man who had all manner of opportunity to make money by letting down the ideal here and there in his business transactions. But he never put through a business deal without conserving the rights of the other man, and effecting an exchange of values between that other man and himself. The sense of elevation in that man's life continued not only in business but in every relation in which he stood. And what is that but religion? What is that but God having his free way in a human heart? Yes, and when a man comes to recognize his sense of exaltation as religion, his doubts cease to worry him because he sees that his doubt is not of religion but of its forms.

In ancient times they built their church and called it their sacred place. It was a great insight.

The object of the church, however, was to teach the sanctity of life in every place. The ancient peoples missed that lesson. They felt they could be religious only when in church. For they located God there.

The modern man, denying that doctrine, has not only repudiated the church but has announced his grave doubt of religion. It was a great gain to discover one sacred place, and the church stands as that achievement. Our next step is the step that Jesus took. It is to see that God is located in the human heart and that all our relations are therefore sacred, because we have the capacity to see them with the mind of God. This is the real experience. It is an elevated spirit that finds inspiration not only through the symbols of worship, but wherever life is set. In a grand sense the whole universe is an exhibition of religion. For everything in the universe looks out beyond itself to some higher source from which its life proceeds. And all things move within the grand purpose and power "whose dwelling is the light of setting suns, and the round ocean and the living air . . . and in the mind of man."

The whole world a religious drama! And man the climax of that drama, having in his heart the power to transcend himself and enter into the rapture of the hills that gives significance to the details of the plains.

Religion, as the sense of elevation in a man's life, thus finds its way into every avenue of our life.

Nothing apart from God and nothing apart from religion. We are apt to think of athletics, for instance, as apart from religion. It can be regarded as such, pursued as such. The athlete can think of himself in terms of his athletic career and the glamour that attaches to the game. But he can also think of the institution or community he represents on the team and the service his good play will render to the same. In the former instance he is a citizen of the plains. In the latter he is a citizen of the hills and has a religious experience as an athlete. We can think of our athletics in terms of the team and the winning of the game. But we can think of it in terms of the physical development of the youth who take part in the game and the state that is benefited thereby. In the former instance we are of the plain country. In the latter we see our athletics religiously.

We are apt to think that education is apart from religion. It can be regarded as such and pursued as such. One of the interesting things on a campus is the spectacle of men who are daily asking questions about religion, often with the implication that religion cannot answer these questions. But the profound answer of religion to a man on the campus is: how about your studies? Don't bother about the inspiration of the Bible, or about whether or not Jesus lived or the miracles happened. Tell me about how you are relating yourself to your studies.

You can regard your career as a student in various ways. You can be very ambitious to excel as a scholar and have a career as such. You can regard your sojourn on the campus as a humdrum thing and say you will be glad when it is over. But while you are there, you can give yourself whole-heartedly to your studies, that you may grow into a bigger and better man and serve the state that has made it possible for you to be where you are. The latter is a religious experience. It is an experience similar to that of him who said: "I will lift up mine eyes unto the hills, from whence cometh my help." So that while questioning religion, you have a chance to test its validity right where you stand in questioning mood. The inspiration of the Bible and the other problems that attach to religion? Once practice religion in the sense of bringing a big and generous spirit to your task of study in hand, and these other matters will eventually take care of themselves. Suppose the Bible were not inspired; you have experienced inspiration. Suppose Jesus never lived; you at least have lived as he is famed to have lived. Suppose the miracles did not happen; you have wrought a miracle in your time and place. Religion for you in this instance does not depend on the Bible or anything else. It depends on how faithful you are to what God wants you to do, and to what you yourself know and feel to be the great, divine thing to do.

This sense of elevation in a man's life takes the form of an insight into the value, and therefore validity, of the forms and ceremonies of religion. Men have put away from them these forms and ceremonies. They see their fellow men at worship and they live surrounded by the religious activities of their community. But they have only a languid interest in the religious program and feel that, lacking the interest in the activities of religion, they are to be excused from taking part in the religious program.

But there is an elevated experience to be reached as we stand in the presence of the religious program. Stop the activities of religion in a community and you take out of that community something that lies near and dear to its heart. Our whole life from day to day, as a community, is colored by the atmosphere of the religious institution. Take the bank out of Chapel Hill and we would be greatly bereft. Take the place of business out and what would happen to us? Take the cafeteria out and what a problem! Take the hotel out and still another problem!

And, indebted to the institution of religion as we are, we take a large and serious contract on our hands when we decide that other men, and not we, are responsible for its welfare. We place ourselves in the position of the man who believes in the necessity of the bank but keeps his money in his own safe. If all the citizens did that, what a step backward would be taken in civilization!

To have this high insight into the forms and ceremonies of religion is to have a religious experience that naturally and necessarily binds us to a joyfully reverent attitude toward these forms. That man honors the religious institution not as a duty but as a privilege, not as an example to his neighbors, merely, but as a chapter in that high living that his nature cherishes and lives by and cannot do without.

The sense of elevation in a man's life takes the form of an insight into the essential nobility, and therefore the sanctity, of human beings. The superficial man—the citizen of the plain country—sees his fellows as they are in all their superficial details and limitations. If they please him, he is pleased to take them into his society. But beholding their failures and mistakes, he regards them as an offense.

> "In even savage bosoms
> There are longings, yearnings, strivings
> For the good they comprehend not."

In every life, however foreshortened, there is a capacity to ascend from where it has continued on the dead level. And when that insight glows on the altar of our hearts, it binds us in a new attitude toward our fellow men. Jesus was accused by the people of the plains of a romantic attitude toward the crude and wicked persons around him. He had a Judas as his disciple. He had a St. Peter who turned traitor in the hour of crisis. All his disciples were unlettered, and some were drawn from the lame and halt and blind of the world of circumstance. But Jesus believed in man because he first had the large and generous view of life. He believed in man because he believed in God.

And he held no suspicions of men. He took them as he found them, giving credit for sincerity, bearing patiently with their infirmities; and when they utterly failed him, he felt the sadness and seriousness of what they did, but was never skeptical of the capacity of human nature. He felt that men were in the making, and, having had temptations of his own, he knew that wrongdoing was a most human thing, to be treated in terms of hope and patience, instead of in terms of repudiation. He knew that to err was human, but to forgive was divine.

Looking at men, men in their daily mistake and sin, he lifted his eyes unto the hills, from whence came his help. He turned his face to God and then to the poor stumbling and fumbling folk around him. And the interesting thing is that our modern psychology, with its study of the human being, has at last by scientific method established the high insight of the Man of Nazareth.

The sense of elevation in a man's life takes the form of an insight into the real nature of pleasure.

He has found something in his life that is preeminently precious and that he cherishes above anything or everything in the world. The old hymn writers felt this.

> "Were the whole realm of nature mine,
> That were a present far too small;
> Love so amazing, so divine,
> Demands my soul, my life, my all."

This is the theme that runs all through the Bible, and especially the New Testament, the joy of the religious experience. "The kingdom of heaven," our Lord declares, "is like a man who, seeking goodly pearls, finds one of great price and sells out all that he has to possess it." Let a man once get a vision of God, let him feel the joy of an elevated thought, and henceforth he will treasure that experience as a pearl of great price. Let that exalted experience become the habit of his life and he will tell you that he carries in his heart the joy that is unspeakable and full of glory. It is the thrill a man feels, only in a superlative degree, when he climbs the mountain and surveys the landscape o'er.

On one occasion the Lord was talking with his disciples on the religious experience, and, after telling them about it in his own great manner, he declared: If you give your hearts to the royal things of the heart and come thus within the sweep of the power of God, this my joy, therefore, in you is fulfilled.

The human being is forever seeking joy. In his seeking, however, his desire goes out to the things that lie on the level of life around him. But his search leaves him dissatisfied in the end. Why? Because he has sought on the lower when he might have sought on the higher level. The real pleasure seeker finds his joy on the higher level, at the right hand of God, where there are pleasures forever more. This man, finding his joy in God, has as keen an interest in the things of the plains as the other man who has not his elevated experience. But all his pleasures on the lower level are touched and hallowed by the one grand passion to serve the highest, to make God real in his heart and thought and will.

Lastly, this sense of elevation in a man's life takes the form of missionary venture.

The program of religion is simply the attempt to open men's eyes to the higher things of which their experience is capable. It is the attempt to bring them to an awareness of their life on its side of power and grandeur and satisfaction, to stir within them conviction. As such the program of religion is essentially missionary. Men who see in the exalted manner are so cheered by their seeing that they want to share it with others. It is beauty felt in the heart and translating itself so that others may enjoy it. The man who has looked upon the face of this altogether lovely world will share it with the Chinese and the Hindoos and the Hottentots. They will share it with their neighbors. The Psalmist had the exalted experience of religion and immediately he proclaims to others: "I will lift up mine eyes unto the hills, from whence cometh my help. My help cometh from the Lord, which made heaven and earth." And then he speaks to others: "He will not suffer thy foot to be moved."

The sense of elevation in a man's life brings with it a conviction of security. "He will not suffer thy foot to be moved." The master passion of the Hebrew people was religion. They saw God. And with their vision of God, they felt secure. As the plains sloping up the hills are guarded by the peaks that tower above them, so the man whose experience soars up the heights has a wonderful strength for the disappointment and failure and trouble of every sort that crowd upon him on the plains. Having brought to them the lofty thought of their meaning, he raises them to their higher power, and they cease to harm him any more. The Psalmist closes with this thought: "I will lift up mine eyes unto the hills, from whence cometh my help. My help cometh from the Lord, which made heaven and earth. He will not suffer thy foot to be moved." "The Lord shall preserve thee from all evil; he shall preserve thy soul. The Lord shall preserve thy going out and thy coming in from this time forth, and even forevermore."

Blessed are the pure in heart; they see God.
                                —Matthew 5:8.

THE GOSPEL means good news. I hope I bring you good news today.

To be pure is to be what we are potentially—what we are intended to be. Everything has a pure side to its life. This must be what the sacred writer meant when, dramatizing the creation of the world, he represents the Creator as saying of each object fresh from his hand that it was very good.

The human being is the de luxe edition of the creative process, and it is beautifully said that when God made us he not only pronounced his achievement very good but declared that we were made so good that we reflected his image. Everything comes into the world endowed with the capacity to give a good account of itself. The acorn may become a good tree; and you and I, having the possibility of goodness within us, may become good men and women.

It is all a matter of desire. We all desire to live the good life. But here is our trouble. There is the lower and the higher, the human and the divine desire. And hence the conflict that is set up within us. Desiring the good life and living the wrong life, we are like the people portrayed in the parable of the sower: "Some seeds," Jesus declares in the parable, "fell among thorns and the thorns choked them out." The minor human desires come in to choke out the good desires. The trouble is we do not want the good life enough. We are not serious about it.

The other day a man stole funds from a bank, and when brought face to face with his deed, he declared that he had not intended to take the money. I am certain he interpreted himself right. But he stole the funds, and it was because his desire for the good life had been to him a vague sort of thing. It had never rounded itself out in his affairs. He had been like the man who dreams of a career in the world of business but does not want it enough to put on his overalls and apply himself to some particular kind of business. He does not want it seriously enough.

This is what is involved in the statement that the way to hell is paved with good intentions. To intend well is one thing, but until our intention is fully formed within us, we are like a seed that is intended to become a tree but that never even so much as gets lodged in the soil. And the injunction of the preacher of a generation ago is still valid: "Give your heart to God." He called for the consecration of desire. It was what Jesus meant when he said: "Blessed are the pure in heart; they see God."

Jesus sought to civilize the emotions. He was different from other teachers before him in this respect. They started with the outside of a man; he started with the inside. They started with methods of goodness; he started by seeking to arouse in men the desire to be good. He was a master of method, but he felt that a method of life must grow out of life, not life out of it. The great Athenian teacher, for example, resorted to the method of knowledge. "If you know what is right," he declared, "you will do the right." And he aimed to give knowledge of how a man should act. There is an echo of this in our modern speech when we express surprise that an educated man should have done wrong. An educated man is a man of knowledge. And he of all men, we say, should behave himself.

Many years ago an Englishman who lived on a Canadian farm encouraged young men to come from the Old World to him to be taught the science of agriculture. When they came to him they insured their lives in his favor, and he murdered them and got the insurance. He was a brilliant graduate of Cambridge University. And when his deed became known, the newspapers were full of the surprise that he, a university man, and one especially with a brilliant intelligence, should have been guilty of murder.

But we do not always live up to our knowledge. And when we do, it is not because of our knowledge. It is because our desire is what it should be.

Jesus believed that knowledge of the good life helped to clarify the good desire. But he first sought to stir the desire. "If any man desires to do God's will, he will know what to do," he said. "Blessed are the pure in heart; they see God." He did not say, "If any man knows God's will, he will desire to do it." Knowledge is a method of life. Purity of heart is a way life takes. "See who you are," he said to those around him. "If you are impressed by the nature you wear, you will want to take care of yourselves. You will want to know about yourselves, that you may the better take care of yourselves."

The men who administered the Roman Empire were interested in the method of doing. "Let the people," they said, "pay their taxes into the treasury. Let them reverence the state and emperor. Let them come together at the Coliseum and make holiday." Thus the method of efficiency was applied even to their recreation.

The men who administered the Jewish theocracy had a similar method of doing. It was distinctly religious doing. "Let the people," they said, "pay their taxes into the sacred treasury. Let them offer sheep or barley, or the lamb, upon the altar. Let them keep the Sabbath. Let them attend upon the Temple service."

Jesus believed in the method of doing. He was continually giving his hearers something to do. And he organized the Christian society so that those who answered his call might have a channel of activity through which to express themselves. But he was not interested merely in doing. He felt that the trouble with the human being lay in his desire. We are in our deeds as we are in our desires. We do as we want to do. And when we do the lower thing it is because our desire for good is not yet vivid enough to take possession of us. Simon Peter, acting disloyally, wanted to be loyal to Jesus. His trouble was that his desire had not yet grown far enough to withstand a break. The tradition is that later he prayed to be crucified head downward that he might prove his loyalty. I am sure that the tradition gives us a correct estimate of his state of mind. And this explains the story of the meeting between Jesus and Simon Peter after the latter's disloyalty. Jesus did not hold his disloyalty against him. He knew that the apostle had wanted to be loyal, but that he had had such a conflict on his hands that his desire was not yet grown enough to handle it. He also knew that Simon Peter, given a chance, would never again repeat his disastrous deed. He had undergone such a transformation. "Be ye transformed by the renewing of your mind, that ye may prove what is that good, and acceptable, and perfect will of God," said St. Paul.

Desire ranges all the way from an interest in a baseball game or a sunset or a social gathering to an interest in the good life. And it was to this latter interest that Jesus always appealed. The gardener realizes that the important thing is to get the seed rooted. And Jesus was like a gardener. He was anxious to get the human being rooted. As I understand him, he never told a man what to do until he first awakened his interest in what was right. "Ye must be born again," he said to Nicodemus.

One day a woman wanted him to give her sons positions in the government she thought he was about to establish. And he asked her if they were ready to be baptized with the baptism that he was to be baptized with. One way of asking the question would be, "Are they fit?" which means, "Are they interested in living the good life?" She was loud in her praises of their efficiency. He believed in efficiency, but he first wanted a man who had the desire to be a man. He knew that whatever that man set out to do, he would do a good, efficient piece of work.

We are strong on doing. "What must I do to be saved?" is a question often on our lips. But salvation is first a matter of being. The being will take care of the doing.

You young people are eagerly asking, "What must I select as my special career in the world?" Jesus would reply, "Seek vocational guidance. It will help you. But be sure to select the career in which you are most interested. That will be the right career for you. And when you select the career in which you are most interested, you will be so interested in it that you will be obliged to carve out a career."

The interest merely in doing is an interest in the outer man. The interest in being is an interest in the inner man. St. Paul tells us that the outer man perishes, and it does. We have seen this very thing happen. In the course of about twenty-five years I have seen it happen in the case of young people who have come to the University. Their parents, in many instances, have been interested in the doing side of those young people's religion. They educated them to learn the Catechism, when they were children, and to go to Sunday School and church. They felt that they had attended to the religious welfare of their children by stressing that outer conformity. Then when they were grown, they left home and came to the University. And, coming to the University, the outer man perished. No more Sunday School or church or religion of any kind. No. The doctrine of Jesus stands, "Blessed are the pure in heart; they see God."

Jesus calls for quality before quantity. We can do all manner of things in the name of living and lack quality in what we do, and the doing is a useless thing. But once the desire for quality is born within us, our deeds stand in splendor.

The good life has three qualities. The first is the passion for the truth. "Blessed are the pure in heart" means, in this instance, "Blessed is the man who has an open, not a prejudiced, mind." "We have the mind of Christ," the great interpreter of Christianity said of the Christians. The mind of Christ in a man is an unprejudiced mind. But how we bristle with prejudices! How afraid we are to let the other man express himself for fear he will upset some cherished belief we have! And how desirous we are to argue with him, that we may show him his mistake! But that is one of the marks of the uncertain mind. And it is one of the three fundamental sins. The good man is obliged to be an open-minded man.

Jesus opened the door of his mind to all comers. He welcomed all views. For he was pure in heart, and to be pure in heart means that we desire only that truth may prevail. And truth is always the unity of opposites. It includes your view as well as mine.

The early Christians were known for their open-mindedness. Even St. Paul, who was a great doctrinarian, wonderfully adapted himself to those with whom he came in contact. He even apologized one day to the High Priest for having transgressed the proprieties in the latter's presence. And there is one instance we all recall in which the early Christians were all of open mind. It was in their relation to slavery. St. Paul actually sent a young man back to his master from whom he had run away, sending a beautiful letter with him that throws light on the relation of the Christians to the slave owners.

They felt that the slave owner had his view of slavery and that the delicate and proper thing to do was to grow men out of the idea of slavery rather than to resort to dogmatism. They had respect, that is, for what the teacher calls the mores.

The good life has another quality. It is the passion for the moral law. "Blessed are the pure in heart" means in this instance, "Blessed is the man who is anxious to conserve the rights of others, even to his own hurt." The Christian is interested in his rights, but he is also interested in other people's rights. And that is the pure life on its moral side. Religion and morality have often been divorced. And hence the spectacle of men and women who, although devoted church members, are turning short corners in business or in their daily treatment of their fellow men. Do to others as you would have them do to you is one of the principles of the New Testament. But so often David Harum's interpretation of this principle prevails: Do to others as they would like to do to you, and do it first.

The doctrine is a popular one that a man cannot keep his friends and tell them the truth or do business and be honest. Then he is better off without friends and better off to fail in business. But Jesus taught the very opposite thing. And there are men and women who in their daily life are illustrating the moral principle. Yes, and there are men who are honest in their business transactions. Not only so, but it could be shown that no great business can succeed by dishonesty.

The early Christians had such a passion for the right that they actually forfeited their lives rather than play fast and loose with the moral principle.

The good life has a third quality. It is the passion for beauty. Righteousness is truth at work. Beauty is the work in its finish, its flower, its bloom. Real beauty is not the formal beauty of a sunset or a flower or a work of art. It is the beauty of the inner life. It is the beauty of the man of generous feeling. "Blessed are the pure in heart" involves in this instance, "Blessed is the man who has a great, generous feeling in his heart for everybody." This is why he has the open mind wherever he goes. He has such a tender regard for others that he is interested in their point of view, and so hesitates to say the word that even gives the suggestion of a sting. This is why he wants to do the right thing by others.

He has such a tender regard for them that he would feel like a lost soul to accept an honor or make money or in any way succeed at the expense of a brother man.

This is the good life in its flowering and fragrance. It is the good life in its excellence. It is the good life in the form of the saint, not the saint with the halo about his brow, but the saint with the sense of beauty in his heart.

The pure, good man, then, is one who has a passion for truth, righteousness, and beauty. And Jesus declares that this is the experience of the blessed life. "Blessed are the pure in heart." Blessed means satisfied. No man is anything but satisfied who lives the good life as Jesus interpreted it, who desires to put quality into his deeds. And no man is anything but dissatisfied when he is short on quality.

We are all in search of the blessed, the satisfied life. And what a lot of mistakes we make in our search. We seek it in money. But very few rich people are satisfied with their life. If they were, they would not be so restless. And when a rich man is satisfied, it is not because of his having money, but because he has obtained it honestly and is using it honestly. And this is to find the blessed life in a life of quality. Honesty is a quality mark.

We seek the blessed life in the form of social prestige. What a lot of human beings are seeking in this manner. But having attained it, let us say, they are still unhappy. Why? Because, perhaps, they have attained it through social climbing, and that is a failure to put quality into what they have done. But whether they have attained the social goal or not, they are dissatisfied because they are short on the qualities mentioned.

Men and women seek the blessed life through education. But education makes not for blessedness of life, but for breadth of life. What a lot of educated people there are who are as dissatisfied with themselves as many of those who are uneducated. They have breadth but not depth of life. Seeking knowledge, they have starved their emotions.

You are all familiar with the story of the man who wrote the book of Ecclesiastes. His book is biographical. And in it he tells us that at one time he sought the blessed life by the way of education. But by and by he declares that this, like other paths he took, led him at last into a blind alley.

Education comes in to enrich the quality of our lives. And the educated man who is religious is a richer specimen of life than the uneducated. But if the religious experience is absent, education will leave us sadly bereft and dissatisfied. It is the absence of quality.

The mark of the blessed life is in a man's own self. And it lies in the quality of his experience, the intense satisfaction he has in what is right. I heard a man say recently that there was only one thing he craved, and that was to be able to say that he had always played the game fair. But that very desire he has now, to roll back the past and play the game fair when he has failed to do so, is what Jesus meant when he said, "Blessed are the pure in heart; they see God." And if he will carry this desire with him into the future, he will find himself in possession of the blessed life that he seeks.

Jesus declares that this blessed life, this life of quality, carries with it the vision of God. I was brought up to think of God as an enlarged physical being. I suppose we were all brought up on that idea. I find that parents are worried when their children ask them about God. They usually invite the preacher to dinner and put the child with his question on him. It is rather an unfair advantage to take of the guest, but parents are human and, besides, the preacher ought to know about this matter even if he does not.

Your preacher confesses to great ignorance when asked to tell a child about God. He is ready also to let the parents work out this difficult problem. I suppose the child must be given the thought about God that is fitted to the child's mind. And it is always the thought of a physical being.

A small boy told me recently that he thought God was the biggest man there was. He has the idea of God as an enlarged physical being. As we grow, however, the day comes when we are not satisfied to think of God as an enlarged physical being. A great many people discard the reality of God altogether as they emerge out of childhood. Jesus found men and women around him at that stage of experience. They were the Sadducees.

Others reach the stage of law. They see law everywhere, and they declare that they are living in a world of law and that there is nothing beyond that. Jesus found men and women who were at this stage of experience. These were the Pharisees.

But he gave a new interpretation of God. There is such a thing, he said, as the pure life, the life committed to quality. And when a man lives the pure life, he has, therefore, a vision of God.

I was brought up on what are called proofs for the existence of God. There was the world, for example. Somebody must have made it who was at least as big as it. Since the world is infinite, it must have been an infinite being who made it. Hence the existence of God. But God, according to that reasoning, is only an inference. And we are not satisfied with an inferential God.

Paley said that we arrived at the existence of God something like this: I find a watch somewhere, and, studying its mechanism, I come to the conclusion that some intelligent being must have made it. The world thus signifies the existence of an infinitely intelligent being who made it. And God is here again set forth as an inference.

One of the old theologians rose for a great utterance when he said that he had in his mind the idea of God, and that the idea called for the existence of the being of whom he had the idea. And God, according to his proof, remains an inference.

I was puzzled over these proofs after I began to reflect on them. They looked all right, but I felt that there was something the matter with them.

One Sunday morning, however, I went to church and heard something from the preacher that helped me tremendously. It is marvelous how we carry the memory of something that impressed us down the years. I can see that little house of God now, resting on one of the hillsides of my father's estate, and I can recall the very words of the preacher that day: "Did you ever realize," he asked, "that when you do something you should do, wanting to do it, you have seen God?" The rest of the sermon I did not bother about, for as soon as the preacher asked his question I began to lay it by the side of these proofs for the existence of God. I was afraid that possibly I was mistaken. And as soon as the sermon was over, I hurried away to be by myself, to see if I had discovered something. And I had. The discovery was that I did not need any proofs for the existence of God if I only had an interest in the pure, good life, in the things that make for quality. That was one instance, at least, when a soul was saved by preaching. Oh, I have to confess that I was not saved at once. For it is not easy for a boy to commit himself to the good life. He is largely a quantitative being, full of action, and not always particular about the quality of his action. But when I reflected on the matter, I always came back to what the preacher said: "When you do a good act, wanting to do it, you have an experience of God."

It is the supreme vision of God and therefore the real beatific vision. Moses, it is said, saw God up on a mountain where the smoke and fire prevailed. I think he had a vision of God, but it was not the clear vision of Jesus, who said, "Blessed are the pure in heart; they see God." There was a lot of the physical mixed up with the vision of Moses. Elijah saw God, it is said, in the whirlwind; later, in a still small voice. And there was the vision of John. Joan of Arc had her vision of God and got things done. There have been all sorts of visions of God. But the desire for the good life in a man is the actual presence of God. And not only does that man see God, but others, beholding him, feel that they look upon the face of the great and beautiful Omnipresence.

This is the story of the Incarnation associated with our Christian religion. Jesus, it has been said, was God manifested in the flesh. I know that this has been interpreted in a physical manner, in the sense that when Jesus was born it was an act of God. But the real story of the Incarnation is this story of a man who was pure in heart. The spirit of purity in a man is the presence of God.

Men do all sorts of things they should not do during the week and on Sunday come to church looking for God. What a great experience it is when we realize that the Kingdom of God is within us, and that when the desire is upon us to live the good life at our place of business, in the kitchen, digging a trench, in a conversation, teaching a class, running a dairy or a laundry, that there God is more splendidly revealed than when he spoke to Moses on the mountain, or Elijah in the whirlwind, and as genuinely revealed as when men, looking on the person of Jesus, saw in him the Incarnation.

When he came to himself, he said . . . I will arise and go to my father.—Luke 15:17, 18.

I AM very happy this morning in the opportunity you have given me of taking part with you in this very important chapter of your life.* And I hope I can say something to you that will be both useful and real. I am certain that if I can say something real it will be useful. I am also certain that if what I say is not real, it will not be useful and will not stay with you long. And by something real I mean something of which you will say: "The preacher told me something about myself." When a man sees what is real, he has a look at what is a part of himself.

The Prodigal Son, whose story you learned when you were children, lived at one time an unreal kind of life and in living that kind of life he was not himself and was a most unhappy youth. But one day he saw what real living was, and Jesus declares

* High School Commencement, 1929.

that immediately he came to himself. Finding reality, he found his own true life and immediately he said: "I will arise and go to my father, and will say unto him, Father, I have sinned against heaven, and before thee, and am no more worthy to be called thy son: make me as one of thy hired servants."

The human being has one supreme passion—the passion for reality.

Young people are being talked about a lot today and they have come in for a considerable amount of criticism. And the criticism is that they are frivolous and even vicious and are bent on everything but reality. In a recent article in one of our magazines they were spoken of as a hell-bent generation.

But every young generation has been severely criticized by the older generation. You will grow into maturity some day, and it is very likely you will be found criticizing the youngsters that surround you. And the more frivolous and reckless you are now, the more severe on the waywardness of youth you are likely to be when you become matured. I have a friend who, when he was your age or a few years older, broke all the commandments, but today he is as hard as nails on the young generation. It looks like sour grapes.

I have been dealing with young people for a great many years—I would not like to tell you for how many years. Methuselah, they say, lived to be nine hundred and sixty-nine years of age. I am sometimes willing to admit that I am ninety-six years old. I do admit it every morning when I awake and begin to stir around. But my point is that having dealt with young people for a great many years, I am here to testify that they are a great race, every bit as great a race as the race that has immediately preceded them, or, for that matter, as any race that has preceded them.

And by that I do not mean that they are perfect. You do not claim to be perfect, do you? They do every day a lot of things they ought not to do and leave undone a lot of things they ought to do. They are lazy sometimes. They are irresponsible sometimes. They squander time and health. They squander opportunity. In this respect, however, they are exactly like their fathers and their mothers before them. But, despite their imperfections, they have the passion for reality. When they seem to have the passion for what is not real, they are indirectly seeking what is real. The unreal seems to be real to them. Hence their apparent passion for the unreal. But, given a chance, they will work it out. For deep down in their hearts is the passion for the real.

The story of the Prodigal Son always comes to our rescue. We are apt to think of him as a youth who was interested merely in what was unreal. But he was really interested in reality, as the sequel to his story reveals. He thought the unreal life he was leading was the real one. Hence his apparent passion for unreality. And how he did swashbuckle around and make a fool of himself! But one day he came to himself and saw what a fool he had been making of himself. He had a vision there of the real, and henceforth he was established in his father's house and behaved himself.

I know I interpret your life correctly when I say that you are serious persons and have deep down in your hearts the passion for reality.

Every man has two capacities. He has the capacity to see his life in a little way, and he has the capacity to see his life in the large. And in saying that you have the passion for reality, I mean that you all want to live in the great way. Nobody wants to make shipwreck of his life. And I am certain that none of you do. But you can misinterpret your life and look at it in the little way. And this morning I want to speak of this danger and to point out the large way in which you may think of yourselves and your life in the world.

You can think of pleasure in the little or the large way. You are young and as such you are full of vitality. Hence your passion for pleasure, and hence the danger that you may look on pleasure in the little way. A young man gets his hands on the automobile wheel and with a group of young people speeds away into the country. What a great time he is having! But in the joy of his venture he steps on the gas and rounds the curves, irrespective of the lives for which he is responsible, irrespective of his own life. The other night a young fellow was driving through Chapel Hill with a group of young people with him, and, in the exhilaration of the road, he was speeding at the rate of seventy miles an hour. But rounding a curve, he ran into a telegraph post and is now languishing in the hospital. If he had had the large view of pleasure, he would have remembered the courteous thing to be done in traveling through a crowded community and would have driven slowly. At any rate he would have remembered that he was responsible for the other lives beside him and would have been careful.

Pleasure all the way through is like that. The way to have real pleasure is to have our pleasure in restraint. Pleasure is like everything else. It has its limits. And if we pass the limit, we pass out of the realm of pleasure into excess. And excess always spells sorrow.

I was brought up on the doctrine that pleasure was a wicked thing and that I was a worldly person in seeking any kind of pleasure. But pleasure is one of the good things, and we are all born to enjoy ourselves. The man who is not getting a lot of fun out of life is making a great mistake. He may seem to himself and others to be a most serious person. But he is not serious so much as overserious. Don't be overserious. Don't become round-shouldered and sad-faced. Straighten up and walk gladly abroad. The whole world is yours. Look it in the face and rejoice. Take it into your heart and enjoy it. But don't run your opportunity of pleasure to the ground. There is more to life than coca-colas and movies and automobiles and dances and late hours. There is the refreshing glass of cold water as well as the coca-cola. There is the happy evening at home as well as the movies. There is the good book as well as the dance. There is the pew in the church as well as the automobile. There is the hour for sleep and rest as well as the late hour. And blessed is the man who has learned to find his pleasure in restraint. That is the real way to have pleasure. It is the great way to look on pleasure. The other way is the little person's way. The Psalmist says, "At Thy right hand, O God, there are pleasures forever more."

Young men and women, these days, have become very frank in their relations with each other. And their frankness has shocked their elders, although the latter likely did many things secretly that the younger generation are doing openly. But there is the little way of viewing the relation between men and women, and there is the large way.

Society is a great old wise person. She may seem to be an old fogy and to place restrictions on young people that are only artificial. But while some of her restrictions are artificial, they are not always so. And the conventions with which she has surrounded the relations of young men and women are rooted and grounded in reality. Let a young man take liberties with the code of chivalry in which he was bred and he will not only do so at his peril but will live to regret his action.

To me there is something beautiful in the frankness of the young men and women of these days. But any beautiful thing can be easily rendered unbeautiful. The rarer the beauty the more in danger it stands.

And the old-fashioned code of purity your fathers and mothers reverenced stands. The beautiful thing we call romantic love is spiritual as well as physical. There is the perfect love here that makes the lower appeal its servant and never allows it to become the master. And the young persons who learn to conserve the sanctity of the other lives around them and the sanctity of their own lives have had a vision of reality that will be to them a benediction in days to come. And I believe you want to have such a benediction resting on you a few years hence. Blessed are the men or women who, looking back over the days of youth, can say that they played the game of romance fair.

There is a little way and a large way in which you may view your careers in the world. Some years ago a young man about to leave our campus gave as his conviction that this thing we call success is all a matter of bluff. The thing to do, he thought, in order to have a career, is to bluff your way along. Go in, in other words, for results, no matter how attained, and the world will make room for you. I had a friend some years ago who was in the business of real estate in the Capital City of our country. He kept a picture of Napoleon on his desk and was fond of repeating Napoleon's saying that God was on the side of the heavy battalions. And every morning he marshaled his heavy battalions on those who were in rivalry with him in the real estate business. And he succeeded. But at what a terrible price! He succeeded, knowing that he had not played the game fair, and knowing that others knew that he did not play the game fair. And, today, in the enjoyment of his money, he is a most unhappy man. Why? Simply because he has not treated himself right. And when a man has not treated himself right, his better self refuses to be satisfied. This man has ministered to the partial and lower side of his nature, but his complete and higher life has been starved, and hence the pangs of hunger that are gnawing at his spiritual vitals. He has taken the meager view of a career and a meager view of a career always ends in dissatisfaction.

There is another meager view of a career. It is the view a young man takes who wants to do big things but who does not want to live up to the conditions by which the big things are to be achieved. He wants to make money or become a great teacher or a great leader. But he does not want to scorn delights and live laborious days. And he does not think of serving his fellow men. His eye is on his own advancement in life.

As I interpret the gospel of Jesus, it has a place for the man who wants to do big things. But it reminds him that nothing is done in the big way that is not of the nature of service. And it reminds him, also, that the way to expand in power is to do valiantly and manfully the little task at hand. I often think of the man who has built up a great business. What a toiler he has been! What a struggle he has gone through to reach his pinnacle of service and fame! And when I hear of a man, like Mr. Duke, who has thus achieved, I say to myself: "He deserves his success."

If any of you young men are going into business, the chance to serve and succeed is as good as that of the business man who has preceded you. But the young man who insists on starting where his successful father left off has it altogether wrong.

"The heights by great men reached and kept
Were not attained by sudden flight,
But they, while their companions slept,
Were toiling upward in the night."

A young friend of mine was graduated some years ago from Emory College, Georgia. He wanted to go into the mill business. The usual method for a young man here is to look around for some influence that will land him in a good position so that he will have a fine salary with which to buy a fine automobile. But this youth put on a pair of overalls and went to work at the lowest and worst paid job in the factory. It is needless to say that he did not buy an automobile and did not spend his evenings racing around. He scorned delights and lived laborious days in that mill and labored evenings studying to become expert in that business. And it is needless to say that today he has a career and is rendering a fine service to the state where he has his career.

It does not matter where you start or what you start at. The chief concern is that you shall start in sincerity and be ready to make yourself necessary in the thing you set your hands to do.

You can take a little view or a big view of religion. Some time ago I asked a young girl who was visiting in Chapel Hill what the church was doing in the community where she lived. She smiled as she said that she did not go to church any more. Being old enough to be her grandfather, I talked with her for a little while about that matter and asked her if she thought she was doing a real and great thing in not going to church. She said by way of excuse that the preacher was dull and the services uninteresting. I then reminded her that this was one of the very reasons why she should call on the preacher and assure him of her readiness to

SERMONS

help him in his difficult work. Surely if ever the church needs us, it is when it is languishing. The preacher is more aware than any one else of his limitations, and you haven't any idea how a happy word from you puts new life into the preacher's heart and into the progress of the church. It is easy to say on Sunday morning: "Well, I guess I'll take to the woods today." It takes a man to sustain the calls of the religious institution.

The age in which we live is full of denials of religion. Well, I am not going to repudiate your denials or tell you what bad people you are in denying the doctrines on which you have been brought up. Doctrine is a growing thing. And I agree with the man who says he does not believe as his father did. But he ought to be able to see farther into truth than his father. He ought to be able to see more to the doctrine on which he has been brought up than his teachers or elders. The man who denies religion because he does not believe what he has been taught about it is not treating his intelligence right.

Suppose everything we have been taught about religion has been false, religion still exists. They thought at one time that the sun went round the earth. Well, it does not go round the earth. The earth goes round it. What a foolish person he would have been who would have said when he found that the sun did not go round the earth, "There is nothing to astronomy." No. The thing to do was the thing that was done. They wrote out a better astronomy.

The Bible admits of clearer interpretation than has obtained in the past. Because you cannot accept what you were told about the Bible does not invalidate the Bible. And the thing to do is not to say there is nothing to the Bible, but to find for yourself a bigger and better Bible.

And the church? Oh, let us grant that it has its imperfections. But so have business and education. Well, suppose I were to write an article and have it published on the passing of business or education. I would have a nice time proving my sanity. Education goes on even if it is inefficiently administered. And business goes forward even if there are highhanded things done in the name of business. And the church has come to stay. And the man who is unable to relate himself to the church stands a witness of his own little view of religion.

Negatives never get a man anywhere. They are the infirmity of little minds. And the religious negation is as foolish as any other negation.

> "He would not make his judgment blind,
> He faced the spectres of the mind
> And laid them; thus he came at length
>
> To find a stronger faith his own."

Some of you are intending to enter the University and I hope you will go on in your studies and that you will be scholars. Some of you, however, may not have that interest, and you have decided to take up the business of life after leaving the High School. And I hope you will have long and happy and successful lives. I hope you will all become rich and that you will all carve out glorious careers. But my great hope for you is that you will have in your hearts the passion for reality and will find your lives on their real side. I hope, namely, that you will all have the desire to see your life in the large way and that you will never be the victims of the meager way of looking at things or events or people. A man can be a scholar and be a very little man. He may be an expert in knowledge and a child in experience. He may be a scientist or historian or mathematician and remain a stranger to the deep and vital and real things of life.

But no great scholar is ever a stranger to the real things of life. If he is not living in a great way, his scholarship is just something tacked on to him, and it is only information he has, not culture. And anybody can read and study and get a tremendous lot of information on any subject. A man may become an administrator or financier or poet or playwright or attain to social prominence, and yet be a little man. But no man can become a great administrator or financier or poet or playwright or be great in the social world who is not great in life.

Be ye wise as serpents and harmless as doves.
—Matthew 10:16.

THE SERPENT has a head full of knowledge. The dove enjoys his experience with life. In the injunction, therefore, of Jesus, the serpent stands for the process of education, while the dove stands for the process of living. Knowledge is imperial. Living is a gentle and co-operative venture. Knowledge is a way of life, and life is richer than any of its ways. When a man has the supreme experience of life, as Jesus did, he is able to say: "I am the way."

The dove has only a partial experience of life. He is not an example of complete living. But life is richer than any or all experiences of life. Living, like that of the dove, divorced from knowledge, is only partial living and results in all manner of foolish things. Knowledge, like that of the serpent, divorced from the gentle art of living, becomes a hard and formal thing. Hence the injunction of Jesus: "Be ye wise as serpents and harmless as doves."

SERMONS

In speaking to you on behalf of your fellow citizens, this evening,* my first task is to congratulate you, as you pass from these sacred precincts to take up your life in our midst; yes, and to congratulate ourselves on your advent among us to carry on with us the task of citizenship. We need your help, and we have been waiting for you to join us on the great campus of life. And having preceded you in that larger sphere of activity, we feel that you look to us for an encouraging word about the responsibility to which you are called.

There is an ancient saying to the effect that many are called but few are chosen. That looks like a hard saying with which to greet the novice at the task of citizenship. But while the saying has been applicable to those who have preceded you, they could have avoided the indictment it contains, and you have it in your hands to avoid the indictment. Down the highway of civilization the record runs: "Many are called, but few are chosen." And yet the message of Jesus is: "I am come that ye may have life, and have it more abundantly." And I am commissioned to say to you that every one of you can find the abundant life and give the denial to the verdict of history that many are called but few are chosen. And the abundant life is nowhere better set forth than in the injunction of Jesus: "Be ye wise as serpents and harmless as doves."

* Senior Vespers, 1930, Dr. Moss's last vesper sermon.

If any of you fail to be chosen in days to come, it will be not because of any arbitrariness in the scheme of things, but because you have not incorporated in your lives the qualities of the serpent and the dove. Nobody is ever rejected who lays hold of the abundant life. The rejected lives have first rejected themselves. The old-fashioned doctrine of predestination wore a frowning countenance. But the doctrine of predestination proclaimed by Jesus is: You are born a unit of life, born, therefore, to grow; and you should find yourself at last like the tree that spreads its protecting branches over the earth.

On one occasion an ambitious woman brought her two sons to Jesus, seeking positions for them in the kingdom he was about to establish. With pride in her heart backing her ambition, she introduced them to Jesus. But as she went on to state the reasons why her sons should be appointed to the coveted positions, Jesus asked her a significant question that she has not answered yet: "Are they ready to be baptized with my baptism?" One way of asking the question is: "Are they fit for the positions they seek? Are they ready for the abundant life?"

The great Darwin coined a saying that has passed into our daily speech, to the effect that life is a struggle for existence in which only the fit survive. In the sense in which Darwin and his interpreters have employed the phrase, the statement needs to be revised. But in a deeper sense, the saying stands. Darwin and his followers have meant that only the smart and strong prevail. But the deeper insight of Jesus was that there is more to a man's life than smartness and the strength that smartness carries with it. And this is the language through which he seeks to convey this deeper insight: "Be ye wise as serpents," but "harmless as doves."

If there was one thing that Jesus did not preach, it was the belated doctrine that the trouble with the world is ignorance and that the hope of the world lies in getting knowledge. That doctrine had been preached before he came, and having been tried out, it had failed. And if he had announced the doctrine, he would have been behind the times.

Every little while in history education has been set forth as the hope of the world. But with all our knowledge the world is not yet saved. And it is significant that the great builders of civilization have seldom been products of the school. The Sophists were schoolmen. Socrates had not had their training. But the name of Socrates, and not the name of a Sophist, remains to this day a household word. The Pharisees were schoolmen. Jesus never went to school. But while we have forgotten the Pharisee, we are singing on the nineteen hundred and thirtieth anniversary of the birth of Jesus that he "shall reign where'er the sun doth his successive journey run."

Knowledge is a necessary and precious and beautiful thing. Jesus and Socrates had knowledge. The difference, however, between them and the others about them who had knowledge was that they interpreted knowledge in terms of living, while the others interpreted living in terms of knowledge. In the one case, life was to yield to what men knew about it. Life was reduced to a formula. In the other, life is richer than knowledge, and knowledge becomes the servant of living. And in the one case, we have an educated man. In the other, we have a man who is educated. An educated man is only a spectator of life. A man with an education is a unit of life and light and joy.

Knowledge comes in to help us in our attempt to be men. It shows us how our life is made. And living, aided by knowledge, is elevated into the supreme experience of the truth, and is thus saved from being a mere romanticism like that of the dove. Yes, and knowledge, aided by living, is likewise elevated into a vision of the truth, and is saved from becoming a hard and fast and formal way of life.

The passion in a man to be a man is what we call by the name of religion. Religion has taken on many forms, and you may have your doubts about the forms it wears. But nobody has a doubt about religion when he sees it as the passion to be a perfect specimen of a man.

Knowledge, therefore, lays the track on which our life is to run, but religion provides us with the steam. There is a lot of steam at work in our lives, but, like the dove, we have not always the track, and hence the foolish things done in the name of living. This state of things has been chronicled in the phrase that we don't know where we're going, but we're on our way. But if we don't know where we're going, we won't fare much better than the dove. Sometimes, like the serpent, we have a good track, but, like the serpent, we lack the proper steam that carries a man forward among his fellow beings.

The dove, having the passion for life, is a very much finer citizen than the serpent. But, lacking knowledge, he is an emotional creature that spends his life only in cooing. If he had the wisdom of the serpent, he would be a very much nobler and more valuable member of society.

The serpent is one of the educated people in the society in which he moves. But he lacks the passion to live among his fellow beings, and, smart as he is, he has to be watched. He knows what he wants, and he wants it when he wants it. The story runs that on one occasion he wrecked the plan of civilization, and he has never been trusted since. What he needs is the quality of life displayed in the dove. If he had that, he would have a high standing among us.

Getting an education, therefore, is an expression

of religion, or it is a very shallow venture. Yes, and in being religious we are showing ourselves to be wise.

Some of you have been studying to be doctors. By and by you will put out your shingle and begin the practice of medicine. And, like the serpent, you have knowledge. If the serpent were practicing medicine, he would be a great man at handing out prescriptions. The doctor who is relying merely on his knowledge has a formula he uses on the sick. When he comes near where they are, he gets out his pad with the formula on it and writes his prescription. The prescription becomes a sort of magical wand that is to set the sick world right. And if you do not get better after taking his prescription, he tells you you are a hypochondriac. It was that kind of a doctor the author had in mind in his statement that when the patient got well God was praised, and when he died the doctor was blamed.

If the dove were practicing medicine, he would do something like the old family physician I once knew, who, lacking knowledge of his science, used to tell his patients that he had had that selfsame malady, but that it gradually left him.

The great doctor studies his patient to learn about his history, his habits, his idiosyncrasies. The last thing he does is to write a prescription, and if he writes one, he does so because he has had an experience with the physical condition of the patient that calls for a prescription. That man not only knows the science of medicine, but enters into the life of his patients. And, in the process, he lays bare the truth, which applied becomes the right thing done. The practice of medicine in his hands is of the nature of religion.

Some of you have been studying here the noble science of law. By and by you will go into the state to put out your sign and begin your practice. Well, like the serpent, you have knowledge. Now your course is clear. But is it?

The man relying merely on his knowledge of the law has a formula he brings to bear on the law court where he defends his clients. The formula is the technicality of the law that he seizes on, if it suits him, or seeks to dodge, if it stands in his way. The technicality of the law is a sort of magical wand, like that of the doctor's prescription, that is to set the world of legal procedure right. This is the little altar boy in the practice of the law. And there are citizens who believe that the only hope for the safety of society from the criminal class is to bring down the law on their heads. But Mr. Osborne, who once administered the Sing Sing penitentiary, said that there was more to the cure of crime than the law; and our late Judge Connor was a great believer in studying the psychology of the criminal.

If the dove were practicing law, he would want

to see the right prevail, but he would seek to impress the jury by sentiment.

The great lawyer knows the law, but, like the dove, he is interested in living. And with this passion to live upon him, he upholds the law in reverence, but is fair to his opponent and eager to arbitrate, that both sides to the issue may have their just deserts. He will defend a corporation. Why not? It is said that corporations haven't any souls. I don't believe that true. But whether his corporation has a soul or not, he has a soul, and, defending the corporation, he will keep on good terms with his soul. With the burning desire for the right, he will do the right, even if he knows that the corporation will dismiss him from its service.

A man of this type practiced law some years ago at the capital of our nation. He was a member of the Christian Church, which may or may not mean anything. The important thing is that he was a member of the society of Jesus Christ, which is founded on the principle: "Be ye wise as serpents and harmless as doves." And when he went into the law court, he brought with him not merely knowledge of the law but the passion to make his knowledge a servant of life. And the practice of the law in the capital of our nation continues to stand in a great debt to that man. The practice of law in his hands was elevated into the region of truth, that applied became the triumph of justice in

SERMONS

the courtroom. The other man is only a lawyer. I am speaking of a man in the practice of law.

Some of you will turn your attention to the great task of industry, and by and by you will be an expert in your field of endeavor. If the serpent were engaged in business, he would be an expert there, but he would have to be watched.

The man of mere knowledge in industry has a formula that he brings to bear on the factory that he operates. The formula is that business is a science and, therefore, a cold-blooded matter of results. And business is a science and a matter of results. Nobody is in business for his health.

The task of industry is a difficult one. For a hundred and fifty years it has had a troubled career, and in the New World we are repeating the industrial sin of the European countries. And this sin is that industry has been a cold-blooded venture of science that disregards the rights of the individual man. The Communist has emerged on the scene with his message of industrial salvation. But the Communist is not the tree that is for the healing of the nations.

If the dove were doing business, he would soon be out of business, for he knows nothing about it. He was never intended for the rugged career of a business man.

The great man in business knows that business is a matter of results, but he is anxious to make his business an exchange of values. He seeks an exchange of values between him and those with whom he does business. He seeks an exchange of values between him and those who toil for him to make his business a success.

The other man is a business man. This man is a man doing business. He brings his knowledge to the people with whom he deals, and the people bring their knowledge to him, and in the process truth is brought to the light and put to work. The truth at work becomes the right thing at work, and everybody is satisfied. And hence his business is of the nature of religion. Jesus was speaking of him when he said: "Be ye wise as serpents and harmless as doves." He was speaking of the other kind of business man when he said: "How hardly shall they that have riches enter into the kingdom of God!" "What is a man profited, if he shall gain the whole world, and lose his own soul?"

The industrial problem is to be in your hands in the days to come, whether you are going to be engaged in industry or not. Industry will get on its feet on this soil only as it gets on its feet in the right way. And the right way will reveal itself when the parties to the strife cease merely to roar at each other about what they know to be their rights, and are ready to arbitrate and find their rights in the white light of truth.

Since the Great War we have had the problems

of international industry on our hands. After the war was over, the nations, sitting around the arbitration board, tried to solve their problem on the basis of knowledge that they offered as a formula for the sick world of industry. Each nation got out its pad and wrote its prescription. The United States had its pad ready and wrote out a prescription to the effect that the other nations were in debt to it and should pay their debt. And this was to treat the sick world of industry with the wisdom of the serpent, but without the passion to live, like that of the dove. And this, I think, explains the era of crippled business that is upon the world at this hour.

If we had had a man in authority during the past few years who was interested in living and who insisted on the truth about the debts, instead of writing out a prescription, business would now be in a flourishing condition. Even in the recent disarmament conference that man was lacking, and the attempt made to adjust the differences between nations took on the nature of a formula. And we know the results.

The differences before that conference were not concerned with how many ships each nation should have. They were concerned with an exchange of values in business. And if the talk had turned on an exchange of values in business, and not on how many ships the nations should have, and if there had been a big enough man present to say, "Let us cancel the national debts and start all over again," the truth of the national differences would have stood revealed and been put to work. Yes, and I am certain that war would have been headed off for a hundred years, and who knows but what it would have been headed off forever?

But I want to say this personal word to you in this parting hour. You are all going out to do one thing in common. You are going to take up your residence among your fellow men. And if ever the statement of Jesus was applicable anywhere, it is applicable in your daily human relations.

The serpent knows about his fellow beings, and he knows that their natures are black, and he applies his doctrine of total depravity to every one he meets. He has thus a certain fixed, formal program of life that he follows, and if his fellow beings get in the way of his program, they are in a bad fix. The world is his oyster. It has to go over to him and meet and sustain his demands. He is as self-righteous in his knowledge of life as a Pharisee and as unrelenting toward any one who varies from his type of knowledge. But even if he had the correct knowledge, which he has not, that would not be the way to proceed. You cannot whip your fellow beings into line with your knowledge. Living is a process and not a hard and fast rule of thumb.

A lot of men and women pursue the method of the serpent. They are as their views, and wisdom will die with them, they think, like the friends of Job. And you are obliged to burn incense to them and their views.

Mothers and fathers have their knowledge of how their children should behave, and rather than fit their knowledge to their children, they would prefer to see their children go ruined and be able to say: "I told you so." Teachers have this way sometimes with their pupils. They are interested in their subject about which they have their knowledge and not at all in the human being to whom they are imparting knowledge. And we need not enlarge on how this imperial serpent of knowledge walks about everywhere, whipping the old world into line. It is ripping good science, this, but miserable lack of living.

The dove, however, is of another mood. His fellow beings are altogether white to him. He shuts his eyes entirely to their frailties. Parents have been known so to sentimentalize their children that the latter grew up to want what they wanted when they wanted it and to be the despair of the community. Women romanticize over prisoners and send them flowers with weak sentiments attached. And there is a lot of the anaemic doctrine about, to the effect that a man is the product of his environment, and, poor fellow, he just can't do otherwise than he does.

"Be ye wise as serpents, but harmless as doves." Human nature is not white. But neither is it black.

It is white with black spots on it. It is, therefore, good in the making. And we neither need to vilify it or be fooled by it. But the man with the passion to live like a man among his fellow beings finds the initial saint in the sinner, the initial good fellow in the apparently hard-boiled, and plants roses in the garden of human relations where thorns and weeds would otherwise infest the soil.

> "I heard a Stock-dove sing or say
> His homely tale, this very day;
> His voice was buried among trees,
> Yet to be come at by the breeze:
> He did not cease; but cooed—and cooed:
> And somewhat pensively he wooed:
> He sang of love, with quiet blending,
> Slow to begin, and never ending:
> Of serious faith and inward glee;
> That was the song,—the song for me!"

The stock-dove does not get far, but he sings the song of living. And, finding the experience of life, he was chronicled by Jesus. We can come into, and sing of, not the experience of a dove, but of a man.

Such was the person of him whose gospel we preach and profess to follow. And he was relating his autobiography when he said: "Be ye wise as serpents and harmless as doves."

PRAYERS

AS THE DAY returns, O God, with its joys and sorrows, its tasks and responsibilities and cares, help us, we entreat Thee, to greet its hours with gladness and so to make the day God's own day.

We are forever conscious of our faults and failures and aware that the wrong we do is our own wrong and not due to circumstance of our fellow beings. We have done those things we ought not to have done and left undone those things we ought to have done. Our hands have marred the divine image with which we have been born. With a deep sorrow in our hearts we recall the slovenly manner in which we have worked and our crude appraisal of things done; the commercial mood that has entered into our friendships and our deeds of service; the impatience with which we have clamored for our rights and the blindness with which we have looked on our duties; the meager way in which we have lived; the hurtful suspicions which we have carried about with us; the rigidness of our judgments and the unyielding stand we have taken for a cause, forgetting that it is better to be right than that any cause should triumph; the ease with which we have taken from our fellows when we were without ability to give in return; and above all, our un-Christlike letting down of the ideal to follow after the path of pleasure and success.

We pray for strength to have our life without marring it; to bear our burdens bravely; to do our tasks with tranquility; to build not merely for the hour but for all time; to give ourselves with such dedication to what we do that our work shall illustrate perfection; to be too great for haste and too high for hate; to love everybody because of the fineness we see in human life despite its limitations; to forgive and still love even when we have been wronged, knowing that the wrong done has been through a lack of judgment and not with the intention to hurt; to have an interest in everything and not to be mere automatons in the world and candidates for mercy and pity when we might be of service to others; to trust our friends, believing that they still love us even when through their blundering they have brought us perplexity and pain; to absorb and not fight our enemies or our enemy conditions; to wish only joy for every one and not to be jealous of those who precede us in achievement or honor; to be champions not of our views but of the truth, knowing that only truth can live and that no criticism can hurt either us or the reality contained in our views; to love without thought of love in return but only for the joy of letting our affections have their uninterrupted way in the world; to replace in our hearts, beauty for ashes, the oil of joy for mourning, and the garment of praise for the spirit of heaviness; to see our life in the largeness of it and to be sad for ourselves when any littleness invades our thought or creeps into our deeds; to have the teachable mind that listens and absorbs truth from any humble source; to learn from our failures and to be frank to confess where we have done wrong or been mistaken; to appreciate always and not to argue; to wish freedom for ourselves and leave others in the enjoyment of theirs; to cultivate sweetness and light and permit no note of bitterness to mar the music of life with its harp of a thousand strings; to be wise and yet to be gentle; and always ready for the comradeship that finds tongues in trees, books in the running brooks, sermons in stones, good in everything, and God in our fellows; that believes all things, hopes all things, endures all things, and sees the Christ-possibility in every situation.

O THOU who dwellest in the pure light of day, and in whom all the objects in the world live and move and have their being; from whom to turn is to fall; to whom to turn is to rise; and in whom to abide is to stand fast forever; grant that this hour spent in the sanctuary may so renew our covenant with life that in the days to come we shall find a strong support when the clouds and darkness gather about us.

WE PRAY, O God, for all sorts and conditions of men, for those who are unemployed that during the severe winter months their families may be provided with shelter and food, and that a great sympathy may be aroused in all our hearts for these, our comrades in the struggle of life, who have fared ill.

We pray for the youth about us that, with the passion for what is young and fresh in their hearts, they may not repudiate the things that have been made sacred with age.

We pray for the matured person with a ripe experience in his life, whose vision carries him beyond the mere world of fact and event, that he may be patient with those who lack his matured outlook, and still trust the new generation of men, even when it might be easy to let the doubt enter in.

We pray for the toiler on the farm, in the mill, on the street, in the kitchen, and in all the varied places where the world's work goes on, that his toil may have the dream of life that shall lift him above the smoke and the grime.

And, O God, we pray for this company of men and women that, having heard the name of Jesus, it may become to us the name above every name, and that, professing to be his disciples, we may make our community radiant with the love that he once spent upon the world.

O GOD, beneath whose guiding hand all the peoples of the earth have their life, and in whom and through whom and by whom we live and move and have our being: we thank Thee for our life in Thee, to whom a thousand years are but as yesterday when it is past, and as a watch in the night. And we reverently beseech Thee that on this day, as we review the past and look out upon the year that lies before us, we may gird up the loins of our minds and be ready to march forward without a fear. And grant that our worship at this time and place shall revive our reverence and courage as we look once more upon the face of the perfect man, Christ Jesus, our life.

WE THANK THEE, O God, for the year through which we have come, for all the happy experiences it brought us, for all its bitter experiences by which we have been schooled, and for the radiant thought still alive among men that we are in the world of God and that, man working with God, all things take upon them a new meaning and hope.

We remember our public and private sins. And

we pray that as the year goes by we may strive to make our government a government of the people, to turn our business into the channel of service as well as of personal gain, to make our education educate, to administer our banking system so that it shall seek to develop every legitimate interest of finance, to administer religion so that it shall be a joy and never a duty or drudgery; and grant that in the year before us men everywhere shall have in their hearts a beautiful renewal out of the springs of life and love and joy.

And to this end we pray that men may come closer to the person of the Saviour of men, and may see in his life, not a strange story of other days, but a story that is intended to be a parable of life— on the street, in the home, and the market place— wherever men live and do business together. So may his kingdom come.

WE THANK THEE, O God, for the day that is at hand, made sacred by the prayers and hymns of those who throughout the ages have felt the stirring of Thy life within. We thank Thee for the men and women among us who greet the day as coming from Thy gracious hand, and who in their hearts have experience of the ancient song: "How amiable are Thy tabernacles, O Lord of hosts! My soul longeth, yea, even fainteth for the courts of the Lord." Grant us all, we beseech Thee, the ancient joy of the Sabbath and of the house of our God. And we pray that our reverent use of time and place this day may teach to us the sanctity of all time and of every place.

AS WE lift up hands of prayer, O God, we beseech Thee for those who are little in their thought of life, their estimate of the world in which they live, to whom the heavens declare only the glory of the astronomer, and to whom the earth is but an opportunity for selfishness and strife. Grant them a glimpse of the world in which the Saviour lived, a baptism of the love he felt, that is creation's final law.

We pray for the poor man that he may be rich in the things of the inner life; and grant that, gradually, through Thy grace and the wisdom and unselfishness of man, the problem of livelihood shall eventually be solved.

We pray for the rich that the great love of Christ may master every desire of their hearts that riches bring. So may they find their joy in creating a better opportunity for their fellow men.

We pray for the moral derelict that love of Christ may visit his empty heart and cause him to cease to do evil and learn to do well.

We pray for all religious men and women that they may have their faith not as a form but as a great conviction. Grant that the Christ may see in them the travail of his soul and be satisfied, and that through them the religious life may make an attractive appeal, the fires of devotion may be rekindled upon the altar, and the church may become as the city set upon a hill.

And grant, O God, to all troubled hearts beauty for ashes, the oil of joy for mourning, and the garment of praise for the spirit of heaviness.

WE REJOICE, O God, in the week through which we have come, the rest of the past night, the sleep that has knit up the raveled sleeve of care, in the glad daylight that is at hand, and in all the joyous relations of the day. We rejoice in the great spacious order in which our lives are set, the mighty temple of Thy spirit, in whom all things live and move and have their being. And we thank Thee for this place, dedicated by the vows of those who built it, and made sacred by the prayers of succeeding generations of reverent men and women. Grant, O God, that as this day we lay the sacrifice of dedicated lives upon the altar, the faith of our fathers may have renewal of its life in our midst.

WE THANK THEE, O God, for all the sacred relations of our life, the joy of home, the love of parents for their children and children for their parents; for our capacity to make friends and enjoy them, and the strength imparted to us by the thought that we are necessary to other lives around us.

We are grateful for the good we see in our fellow beings and for our ability to see past their mistakes to their good intentions, and for all the rare beautiful persons about us who, because of the love that is in their hearts, think no evil of life, but believe all things, hope all things, and endure all things.

And we pray that when human hearts are bereft of the spirit of love, they may be born again; that all the envies and hates and suspicions may be gradually banished from our lives, and that love such as stirred the heart of Jesus may have its perfect way among us.

We pray for the sick that they may be restored to health, and, especially, for the sick in mind, that they may find the health of a serene and emancipated outlook upon the world.

We pray for those who are easily led in the way of temptation, to whom the path of dalliance is an inviting spectacle, and who are conscious of having tampered with their moral heritage, that, like the ancient prodigal, they may come to themselves.

We pray for the fathers and mothers of the state and their children at home and abroad, that the older may learn to be patient with the younger generation, and that youth may have a sense of reverence for age.

And we pray for men everywhere that, toiling in

the fields of material values, the fires of reverence may continue to burn upon the altars of their hearts, and that daily they may lift up their eyes unto the hills, from whence cometh their help.

WE ADORE THEE, O God, as the source from which our lives proceed, and we lay upon the altar today our gratitude for life, and our penitence for the trivial and irreverent use we have made of our gifts.

For the seasons in their annual round, each bearing its sweet beatitude to our doors, we render unto Thee our heartfelt thanks. We rejoice in the great abounding world and are grateful for sun and shower, for meadow and hill, for the tender growing things nurtured by the gentle principle of life, which are lent out of Thy silent and beneficent generosity.

We are mindful of the homes where we have been reared, and of the tender tie that binds the parent to the child, the children to the parents and to each other. And we pray that as around the sacred hearth the citizens of this beautiful commonwealth gather during the present week, the fires of love and joy may be rekindled there into a sacred flame.

Grateful for the friends that bless us with their confidence, their love and hope, we pray that we may all be worthy of the friends who give us their hearts, and that through us they may find the journey of life an easier thing.

We thank Thee for the citizenship we have upon this soil where a noble history has been wrought, for the men and women with dreams in their hearts who have gone before us, and the heritage we have in the memory of their precious and beautiful way of life. And we pray that the torch of idealism received by us from them may in our hands shed an added radiance abroad. So may the generation that pre-empts the land today lend to posterity a legacy of faith and integrity that shall make for renewals of reverence.

Bless the child and the old person, and in Thy gracious providence gently guard the young from doing harm to themselves before they are grown. Grant that all poor and struggling folk, despite the hard circumstances of their lives, may have a rich experience of Thy tender care. And we pray that the wheels of industry, blessing our country with prosperity, may slowly merge out of the hard sound of materialism into the music of justice.

O GOD, we adore Thee as our life, precious, wonderful; and we rejoice that we need not search for Thee in the heavens above or the earth beneath, but that in Thee we live and move and have our being.

We thank Thee that every sight and sound carries with it hint of larger, diviner reality, and that every trivial relation in which we stand is sacramental, if we have our hearts exposed to the glory that is there.

And we humbly entreat Thee that, as the winds come to us from distant and mysterious realms, we may also feel the breath of Thy spirit that "bloweth where it listeth" and extends everywhere; as night approaches and the wearied toiler seeks the rest and joy of home, so in all the dark experiences of the soul may we turn to our home and peace in Thee; as the morning breaks and our bodies are refreshed for the day's task, may our spirits emerge, strengthened for the day's worry and care, in Thy abiding presence; as on this day we pause to reflect and renew the covenant with life, may the abundant life reveal itself unto us and may we find enlargement of thought and purpose for days to come.

WE INVOKE THEE, O God, in behalf of all the weak and helpless folk in the world, and especially such as are known to us from day to day. Rejoicing in the privilege in which we stand, grant us to feel and practice the duty of our privilege. In our culture, we pray that we may possess the rare and real culture of the heart that welcomes the untutored person for a brother man. In the social wellbeing we enjoy, grant us a gentle and courteous feeling toward those who stand in social obscurity.

Heirs to the good and happy things of life, we beseech Thee for the reverent mind of Jesus that remembers the poor, and is stirred not merely by the passion to have but by the passion to share.

O God, we thank Thee for the beautiful gift of life. Deliver us from the partial interest in living, from every form of enjoyment that kills, from every triviality of mind and heart and will. Grant us to live in the beautiful manner of him who came that we might have life and have it more abundantly.

WE ADORE THEE, O God, as our life and our abiding security. Grant us to enter into the joy of Thy presence.

As the day returns and with it the mighty procession of the Spirit in which all things live and move and have their being, help us to feel the sense of permanence and to know that underneath all the changing world are the everlasting arms.

As the trees toil upward and wave their branches to the heavens, may our thoughts also rise above the littlenesses of our local world into the place of central calm.

As every little object toils to maintain itself in the sun and has comradeship with other lives, so may we each, working out our destiny, sense the struggles of others and be ready to serve as well as to receive.

As every living thing has its purpose and the capacity to realize the end for which it was made, so may we seek to know and prize our life; and as day unto day uttereth speech, may we quietly fulfill our destiny.

As in the sacred book we read of one who came that we might have life and have it more abundantly, grant that we may learn of him, the gentle and lowly in heart, that we may find the peace of which he spoke and possess the wealth and joy of life with which he has blessed the centuries.

WE THANK THEE, O God, for this company of goodly folk, and for the men and women on this campus who are seeking the larger horizon.

We thank Thee for the teacher, the pupil, the parent, and the school, and that in every community in the land the lamp of truth is trimmed and burning, and that through its kindly leading we are slowly passing beyond our ancient obsessions and becoming an enlightened people.

And we pray that, led by the light, our search may carry us forward until at last we find the true light that lighteth every man that cometh into the world; that, in coming to know, we may likewise learn to feel the inherent splendor of our life, and the passion may be upon us to walk worthily of this splendor there revealed.

So do we pray to be delivered from the culture

that, priding itself on knowledge, lacks the experience of the things that make for good will and sweeter relationships among men. So grant that out from the school may radiate the ambition to live and to serve, and that every community, great and small, may become a center of co-operation and beautiful and happy living.

We pray for the cause of education everywhere; for the schools of our state and the Commonwealth; for the President of the United States, the Governor of our state, and all who are called to rule among us. Grant that the Nation, rich in its products and material well-being, may stand rich in its power to generate men who shall be saviours of their fellow men.

www.ingramcontent.com/pod-product-compliance
Lightning Source LLC
Chambersburg PA
CBHW021123300426
44113CB00006B/270